English for Business

Teacher's Resource Book

Ivor Williams

Australia • Canada • México • Singapore • United Kingdom • United States

**English for Business
Teacher's Resource Book**

Ivor William

VP, Director of Content Development: Anita Raducanu
Director of Product Marketing: Amy Mabley
Editorial Manager: Berta de Llano
Director of International Marketing: Ian Martin
Development Editor: Margarita Matte
Editorial Assistant: Jason Siegel
Production Project Manager: John Sarantakis

Interior Design/Composition: Miriam Gómez
Cover Design: Miriam Gómez, Miguel Angel Contreras
Printer: West Group
Printed in the United States of America

Copyright © 2007, by Heinle. Thomson, the Star logo, and Heinle are trademarks used herein under license.

Printed in the United States of America.
1 2 3 4 5 6 7 8 9 10 — 10 09 08 07

For more information contact Heinle ELT, 25 Thomson Place, Boston, Massachusetts 02210 USA, or visit our Internet site at elt.thomson.com

All rights reserved. No part of this work covered by the copyright hereon may be reproduced or used in any form or by any means—graphic, electronic, or mechanical, including photocopying, recording, taping, Web distribution or information storage and retrieval systems—without the written permission of the publisher.

For permission to use material from this text or product, submit a request online at http://www.thomsonrights.com

Any additional questions about permissions can be submitted by email to thomsonrights@thomson.com

ISBN-13: 978-1-4240-0011-1
ISBN-10: 1-4240-0011-4

Contents

Introduction	iv
Teacher's Notes	2

Photocopiable Materials

Additional Activities
Unit 1	72
Unit 2	75
Unit 3	78
Unit 4	81
Unit 5	84

Reading Resources
Unit 1	87
Unit 2	89
Unit 3	91
Unit 4	93
Unit 5	95

Writing Resources
Unit 1	97
Unit 2	99
Unit 3	101
Unit 4	103
Unit 5	105

Unit Tests
Unit 1	107
Unit 2	110
Unit 3	113
Unit 4	116
Unit 5	119
Answer key	122

Introduction

English for Business is a four-skills course designed to build both fluency and accuracy in tertiary students enrolled in business programs. By setting language activities in the context of their future professional lives, it motivates learners to develop the language skills they will need for success in their careers.

Program components
- Student Book
- Teacher's Resource Book
- Audio CD

Organization of the Student Book
The five units of the **English for Business** Student Book focus on five fundamental areas of business:

- Making your way: making career choices, preparing a resume, applying for a job, job interviews

- Selling is what it's all about: jobs in sales, sales techniques, analyzing sales data, dealing with customers, dealing with complaints, e-commerce

- Marketing the product: advertising, brands, market research, marketing strategies, marketing life cycles

- Financial Matters: personal expenses, bank accounts, managing expenses, economic issues, investments

- Global Concerns: cultural issues, corporate culture, changes in the workplace, global perspectives

Every unit contains six two-page lessons, integrating the four language skills and reviewing and extending grammar points that students have previously studied. For every unit, there are a number of listening activities, reading passages, and writing activities. Students have numerous opportunities to practice and improve their communication skills, including role plays, pair and group discussions, and whole-class speaking activities. Every unit culminates in a Team Project, in which groups utilize their ideas and language skills together to produce a tangible product such as a dossier, a report, or a multimedia presentation.

Contents of this Teacher's Resource Book

This Teacher's Resource Book contains everything you will need to successfully teach **English for Business** and adapt it to the specific classroom needs of your students.

For each unit of the Student Book, you will find the following:

- Detailed teaching notes for each lesson. Instructions are given for presenting every activity in the classroom, and answer keys are provided following each activity, for easy reference.
- A photocopiable Additional Activity for each lesson, giving further practice in objectives from the lesson.
- Photocopiable reading texts plus activities in the Reading Resource, related to the theme of the unit. These readings broaden the scope of the unit to include material not specifically covered in the Student Book.
- Two photocopiable writing activities in the Writing Resource, designed to build and reinforce students' skills at the paragraph level. Among the objectives practiced are generating and organizing ideas, writing topic sentences, and paragraph unity. In addition to single paragraphs, these tasks give practice in useful writing formats such as articles, reports, advertisements, essays, material for manuals, etc.
- Teaching notes for the Extra Activities, Writing Resource, and Reading Resource incorporated into the unit notes, in the suggested place for each activity in the unit sequence.
- A two-page photocopiable Unit Test, along with role cards and a script for assessing students' listening and speaking ability.

Unit Tests

Each Unit Test checks understanding and mastery of the grammar, lexis, and language functions presented in the corresponding unit. Each test follows the same sequence:

- The first four to six exercises cover grammar and lexis in a variety of exercise formats including matching, error identification, multiple choice, etc.
- The next section, consisting of one or two exercises, covers listening, with a script provided for the teacher to read aloud.
- The final exercise is an optional speaking activity that tests fluency and the use of appropriate language through a role-play activity for pairs. Photocopiable role cards are provided.

With the speaking section included, the test comprises 50 points. Without the speaking section, the test comprises 35 points.

The purpose of this book is to empower business students with the language and life skills they need to carry out their career goals. To this end, it provides ample opportunities for students to build awareness of and practice in language in real-life scenarios. Its integrated skills approach develops students' self-confidence to survive and succeed in professional and social encounters within an English-speaking global community.

Unit 1

Making your way

Objectives

Language skills: discussing and evaluating ideas, listening and reading for specific information, understanding vocabulary in context, listening to and understanding a telephone conversation, listening and taking notes, identifying key ideas in a text, summarizing information, reading for the general idea, identifying formal and informal registers

Functions: making suggestions and recommendations, expressing opinions, giving reasons

Grammar: verb / noun collocations, phrasal verbs with *fill*, modals for obligation, recommendation, etc., connectors, phrases with *make* or *do*

Lesson 1 Time to make a decision   SB Pages 2–3

This lesson deals with the subject of career choices and how to go about finding a job. It includes discussion activities, listening comprehension activities, and reading comprehension activities. The listening activity presents suggestions for finding a job and vocabulary. The reading activity focuses on job ads and leads into vocabulary practice. The lessons finishes with a discussion activity in which students share and compare opinions.

a
- With books closed, ask students to share information about people they know who are looking for a job or who just found work. Invite them to talk about what the people they know did / are doing to find a job.
- Have students open their books. Read aloud the suggestions. Then organize students into pairs and have them discuss which suggestions they agree with and why.
- In a whole-class discussion, invite students to share and explain their opinions.

b CD T-1
- Ask students to look at the photograph. Elicit that the two people are students and that they are talking about job hunting. Have students listen to the conversation once through without making any notes.
- Ask students to read the list of ideas in their books. Then have them listen to the conversation again and check the suggestions that are mentioned. Check answers.
- Invite students to comment on the relative merits of the suggestions in the list.

> **Answers**
> think about your specific interest in business, identify strengths and weaknesses in the area of business, look at some ads and see what is available, consult with different companies and find out what is required in each department, visit the college counselor and discuss

c
- Read aloud the sentence openers in the box. Elicit or point out that all of these phrases can be used to make a suggestion. Choose one of the phrases and read it aloud again. Elicit ways of finishing the sentence with appropriate suggestions about how to start looking for a job.
- Arrange students in pairs and have them take turns making suggestions using the phrases in the box plus any other suitable phrases they know.
- Finish up the activity by asking pairs of students to share their ideas with the rest of the class.

d
- Ask students to look at the texts. Elicit that they are job ads. (If necessary, clarify that *ad* is an abbreviation of *advertisement*.) Ask students where ads like this are typically found.
- Ask students to read through the ads in silence. Then read aloud the instructions and have students read the ads again and underline the skills and qualifications that are needed for each job.
- Point out to students that highlighting key information about skills and qualifications is a useful procedure to follow when comparing ads for different jobs. Check answers.

> **Answers**
> **Secretary / Receptionist Skills:** proficiency in MS office, good interpersonal skills, good telephone manners
> Qualifications: diploma from a recognized business school
> **Accounts Manager Skills:** take responsibility for existing accounts, develop new business
> Qualifications: graduate, proven ability in accounting
> **Sales Representative Skills:** enjoy all aspects of sales, ability to work in a team, strong interest in client
> Qualifications: none needed

e
- Read aloud the first question and elicit the correct answer.
- Then have students work alone or in pairs answering the rest of the questions. Check answers.

> **Answers**
> 1. A diploma from a recognized business school. 2. Responsibility for a number of key existing accounts and the development of new business. 3. Experience not a necessity. 4. No, but it is preferable. 5. The on-the-job training and the commission on car sales.

f
- Read aloud the first sentence and elicit the correct answer, making clear to students that the missing word can be found in one of the three job ads.
- Then have students work alone or in pairs completing the rest of the exercise. Check answers.
- At this point, review any doubts that students may have regarding items of vocabulary in the job ads. Explain, for example, that *remuneration* is a formal word meaning one's pay or salary.

> **Answers**
> 1. negotiable 2. essential 3. advantage 4. necessary

g
- Organize students into pairs and have them discuss and compare the relative merits of the three jobs advertised in the ads. Remind students that some of the reading comprehension questions mention advantages that some of the jobs offer.
- Ask pairs of students to get together in groups of four and have them share and discuss their ideas. Then open up the discussion for the whole class.

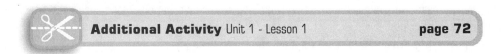
Additional Activity Unit 1 - Lesson 1   **page 72**

Answers
1 1. qualifications 2. salary 3. duties 4. candidate 5. negotiable 6. benefits 7. skills 8. experience 9. recruitment agency 10. counselor
2 Answers will vary.

Writing Resource 1A   **page 97**

In this activity, students write a job advertisement similar to the ones in Lesson 1. They will select one of the posts to write about. In their ads, they include the qualifications, skills, and experience required for the job along with the duties and responsibilities that the job involves.

Lesson 1

Lesson 2 Following through

SB Pages 4–5

In this lesson, students look at some of the practical steps that they can take when looking for a job. They complete, listen to, and then practice a telephone conversation. Students then study language commonly used in resumes and then they listen to the advice of a career counselor. The lesson ends with a discussion activity in which students share and compare opinions.

a
- With books closed, ask students if they can recall the conversation they listened to in the previous lesson between Martha and John. Remind students that one of the things that they decided to do was to call to make an appointment to speak with the college career counselor.
- Ask students to open their books. Read aloud the discussion questions. Then organize students into pairs or small groups to discuss them. Finally, open up the discussion for the whole class.

b
- Direct students' attention to the photograph and the telephone conversation. Elicit or point out that the photograph shows Mrs. Mills' personal assistant (PA).
- Read aloud the opening exchange between Martha and the PA. Then have students work alone or in pairs reading and completing the rest of the conversation using the expressions in the box.

c (CD T-2)
- Ask students to listen to the audio to check their answers.
- Draw to their attention the use of indirect questions such as *Can I ask why you are calling?* and *May I ask who is calling?* Ask students to say how they would ask for this same information using simple, direct questions *(Why are you calling? Who is calling?)* and then talk about the differences between the two forms. Elicit or point out that the indirect question form is more formal and polite.

> **Answers**
> 1. d 2. b 3. e 4. a 5. c

d
- Organize students into pairs and have them practice the completed conversation. Make sure each student takes a turn doing each of roles.
- Invite pairs of students to present the conversation for the rest of the class.

e
- With books closed, ask students what a resume is. Elicit or explain that the word comes from the French verb *resumer*, which means to summarize, and point out that the word is sometimes spelled *résumé*. Also, elicit or explain, that another (British English) term for resume is *curriculum vitae* (or C.V.), an expression from Latin meaning "the course of one's life".
- Ask students to open their books and to look at the words and phrases in the box. Then direct students' attention to the chart below where expressions are sorted into different categories. Read aloud the first item in the box and have students say which category they think it belongs in.
- Then have students work alone or in pairs sorting the remaining words and phrases into the correct categories. Check answers.

Unit 1

Answers
personality: efficient, hard-working, independent
skills: familiar with Microsoft Office, competent in conversational Spanish, fluent in French, knowledge of the Internet
qualifications: high school diploma, diploma in computer science, B.A.
hobbies / interests: swimming, theater and film

CD T-3

f
- Remind students about Mrs. Mills, the college counselor whom Martha made an appointment to see. Elicit ideas about what a college counselor does and how a college counselor can help students start to look for work.
- Ask students to listen to the audio once through without making any notes. Then, draw their attention to the incomplete notes to the right. Have students listen again and complete the notes. Remind students to write just key words and phrases. Check answers.

Answers
Looking for a job: . . . training and qualifications
Business: . . . particular strengths and what you do not enjoy doing
Human Resources: . . . match person with position, recruitment, staff development, welfare, motivation
Sales & Marketing: . . . focus on convincing the customer to buy
Finances: . . . calculating expenses, profits, salaries, investment

g
- Read aloud the instructions. Then give students some "thinking time" and have them make notes about the qualifications, skills, and personality traits that are required or that are particularly important in their chosen job.

h
- Read aloud the sample text in the notebook paper. Then draw students' attention to the phrases that can be used for expressing opinions or for giving reasons. Elicit additional phrases.
- Organize students in pairs and have them share, compare, and discuss their ideas from the previous activity. Encourage them to use the language in the chart.
- Finally, open up the topic for a whole-class discussion. Encourage comment and debate.

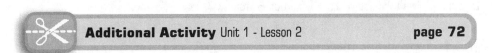
Additional Activity Unit 1 - Lesson 2   page 72

Answers
1 1. b 2. c 3. a 4. c 5. b 6. c 7. a

Reading Resource 1A   page 87

This reading is about two young graduates who turn their own job hunt into a job. Students answer various comprehension questions and use contextual clues to understand idiomatic expressions featured in the text.

Answers
A Answers will vary.
B 1. Dave Rosen and Alan Bailey graduated two years ago after . . . 2. Using their knowledge of business and their computer skills, . . . 3. They felt a bit disheartened and even thought about calling it a day. 4. Soon after launching the site, they were pleasantly surprised to receive . . .
C 1. with flying colors 2. a dog's breakfast 3. like hot cakes 4. take matters into their own hands 5. calling it a day 6. have it made 7. make a go of it 8. off the ground 9. an uphill struggle 10. kicking our heels

Lesson 2

Lesson 3 Filling out forms

SB Pages 6–7

This lesson is about another important aspect of job-hunting, namely, filling out forms. Students work with some high-frequency collocations of verbs with noun phrases before completing a gap fill reading activity. They then focus on phrasal verbs derived from the verb *to fill*. The lesson ends with a listening comprehension exercise and a discussion activity.

a
- With books closed, elicit verbs that are frequently used with the noun *application*, i.e. an application for a job. Ask: *What does a person looking for a job do with an application? What does a company do with applications?* Try to elicit verbs like make, submit, receive, process, etc.
- Ask students to open their books and have them read the instructions and the examples carefully. If necessary, explain briefly the idea of collocations - words that are often used together in relatively fixed combinations.
- Organize students into pairs and have them combine the verbs from box A with the noun phrases from box B to produce appropriate collocations. Check and discuss answers.

Answers
make decisions, proofread your application, short-list candidates, submit your application, apply for a job, fill out the application form, follow instructions, follow the same steps, leave a section blank, list your abilities and skills, list your most recent jobs

b
- Draw students' attention to the photograph. Elicit or point out that the young woman is filling out an application form for a job. Then have students skim through the text quickly to grasp a general idea of its contents.
- Ask students to read the text again, more carefully this time, and to complete each space with the correct word. Point out that the words they need in order to complete the text all come from the previous exercise. Check answers.

Answers
1. apply 2. submit 3. short-list 4. list 5. fill out 6. follow 7. leave 8. apply

c
- Ask students to work alone summarizing the two ideas in the notes with just the key information.
- Then have students compare and discuss their answers in pairs. Check students' answers.
- Finally, invite students to comment on the information in the text and encourage them to offer additional ideas or suggestions.

Answers
Makes comparison between candidates easier, Makes it easier to short-list candidates
Read the form carefully, Answer each question honestly and accurately

d
- With books closed, ask students what they know about phrasal verbs. Elicit or clarify that a phrasal verb is a compound verb made up of a base verb combined with a particle, which is usually a preposition but can also be an adverb. Discuss the fact that the meaning of a phrasal verb cannot always be deduced from the meaning of the individual words from which it is formed. Elicit some examples of phrasal verbs.
- Ask students to open their books and to read the first sentence. Elicit the correct answer. Then have students work alone or in pairs completing the remaining sentences with *up* or *in*. Check answers.

Answers
1. in 2. up 3. in 4. up

Unit 1

e
- Referring to the answers of the previous exercise, draw to students' attention the fact that there are a number of phrasal verbs that have more than one meaning. Also, remind students that not all phrasal verbs "behave" the same way. For example, some have no object, some can be divided by an object or an object pronoun while others cannot. Read aloud the first item from the list on the left and elicit the correct definition.
- Then ask students to work alone or in pairs completing the rest of the exercise.
- Check answers and focus students' attention on the small but significant difference between the meaning of, for example, to *fill up* with an object compared with to *fill up* without an object.

Answers
1. b 2. d 3. c 4. a

f
- Read aloud the first sentence and elicit the phrasal verb based on *to fill* that best completes it.
- Then have students work alone or in pairs completing the remaining sentences with the correct forms of the correct phrasal verbs. Point out to students that it may be necessary to make changes to the verb tense of the phrasal verb. Check answers. At this point, it may be useful to mention that in British English, people typically *fill in* rather than *fill out* an application form or other types of official forms.

Answers
1. fill him in 2. fills up 3. fill in 4. filled up 5. fill in

g
- Provide students with some examples of common phrasal verbs that have more than one meaning, for example, *to take off*. This can mean *to remove*, as in *I took off my jacket.* or it can mean *to leave the ground*, as in *The plane took off*.
- Encourage students to observe the use of phrasal verbs in texts that they read inside and outside class and to keep notes of the meaning (or meanings) of each one and how the verbs are used.

h
CD T-4
- With books closed, remind students of the listening material they worked on in the previous lesson in which Mrs. Mills gave Martha and John some advice. Focus students' attention on the idea of strengths and weaknesses, which Mrs. Mills touched upon in her talk. Elicit or make clear the idea that these two words express contrasting ideas.
- With books still closed, have students listen to the conversation once all the way through for the general idea. Then ask students to open their books. Have them listen again and complete the table with notes about Martha and John's respective strengths and weaknesses. Ask students to compare their answers with those of a classmate. Then check answers as a whole class.

Answers
John's Strengths: good at networking, good with people **Weaknesses:** organizational skills, lazy
Martha's Strengths: organizational skills, drive and enthusiasm **Weaknesses:** impatient

i
- Organize students into pairs and have them share ideas about their respective strengths and weaknesses. Encourage students to think of ways of presenting weaknesses or deficiencies in such a way as to make them sound less serious.
- Invite students to discuss this topic as a whole class.

 Additional Activity Unit 1 - Lesson 3   page 73

Answers
1. 1. out 2. in 3. in/out 4. for 5. at 6. up 7. up 8. down 9. about 10. in
2. Answers will vary.

Lesson 4 Preparing your resume

SB Pages 8–9

In this lesson, students look more closely at how to prepare a good resume and what to include in it. The lesson begins with discussion, reading, and listening activities. The language focus for the speaking activity is on phrases—in particular, sentence openers—that are used for giving advice and for making recommendations. Students then read the resumes of two applicants for a job and evaluate the strengths and weaknesses of each candidate. Students then listen to a conversation and take notes of key ideas before writing their own resumes.

a
- With books closed, remind students of what they discussed in Lesson 2 regarding resumes. Invite students to share ideas and comments about resumes. Ask them if they or anyone they know have ever prepared a resume.
- Ask students to open their books and to read the statements about preparing a resume. Working alone, have them read the suggestions and write whether they agree or disagree with each one. Then organize students in pairs and have them compare and discuss their answers. Open up the discussion for the whole class.

b
- With the whole class, discuss the importance of planning and preparing a resume carefully. Then ask students to work alone reading the steps and numbering them in the best order.
- In pairs, have students compare and discuss their answers. Then check answers with the whole class. At this point, deal with any questions that students may have regarding vocabulary items.

Answers
5, 6, 1, 2, 4, 3

c CD T-5
- With books closed, elicit ideas about the activities and responsibilities of a human resources manager. Then tell students that they are going to hear a human resources manager giving some advice about what to include in a resume.
- With books still closed, have students listen to the audio once all the way through for the general idea.
- Ask students to open their books and to read through the list of items. Then ask students to listen again and to check the items that they think should be included and to place a cross next to the ones that they think should not be included. Check answers.

Answers
To be included: address, education, references , e-mail, experience, interests, volunteer work

d
- Draw students' attention to the expressions in the box. Review and discuss the various ways of making suggestions and recommendations. Make sure that students understand that "not have to" is used for talking about things that are optional rather than obligatory.
- Arrange students in pairs and have them take turns summarizing the advice offered by the human resources manager in the audio. Encourage students to experiment with language using the phrases in the box to express the human resources manager's points in their own words.

- With books closed, elicit places where job advertisements are commonly found. Write a list of students' suggestions on the board. Then elicit ideas about the sort of information that is typically included in a job advertisement.
- First, have students read through just the job ad. Then invite observation and comment about the job. Encourage students to say what they think the job would involve.
- Then direct students' attention to the two resumes below. Have them consider each candidate's strengths and weaknesses and try to decide which of the two they consider to be better suited to the job advertised.
- Have students compare and discuss their choices in pairs.

CD T-6
- With books closed, start a discussion about what students think happens to a person's resume once it has been received by a company. Ask: *Who reads the resumes? Which people make decisions about hiring? How do they come to a decision?*
- With books still closed, tell students that they are going to hear two people discussing the relative merits of the two applicants from the previous exercise. Have students listen to the conversation once through for the general idea.
- Ask students to open their books and to look at the notes in the chart. Have them listen to the audio again and check the positive points that are mentioned about each of the two candidates. Check and discuss answers.

> **Answers**
> Applicant 1: years of experience, range of responsibilities
> Applicant 2: overall qualifications, experience related to finance

- Review the ideas and advice offered in this lesson about preparing a resume. Refer students back to previous exercises and elicit ideas about what information should and should not be included in a resume and in what order.
- Then have students work alone drafting their own resumes. After that, encourage students to work in pairs reading through each other's work and suggesting corrections, additions, deletions, and any other improvements.
- If students are comfortable with the idea, their resumes can be collected in a class dossier or they can be displayed around the walls of the classroom.

 Additional Activity Unit 1 - Lesson 4   **page 73**

Answers
1. 1. Personal characteristics 2. Education 3. Skills 4. Experience 5. Extracurricular

2. Answers will vary.

Lesson 4

Lesson 5 Sending it all off   SB Pages 10–11

This lesson covers another important step in the job-hunting process, the cover letter that accompanies an application for a job. Students begin by considering the important matter of formal and informal registers both in spoken and in written English. Students then focus on the use of connectors to add cohesiveness to their writing. The lesson ends with a listening task on the subject of e-mail etiquette and a writing activity.

a
- With books closed, introduce and explore the topic of formal and informal registers in speech, both in English and in the students' first language. Elicit observation and comment about the various ways that they address people of different ages, of different social backgrounds, etc. Encourage students to give examples from their own language to illustrate the appropriate use of a formal register in a given situation.
- Ask students to open their books and to read through the statements. Read aloud the first statement and ask: *Is this formal or informal?* Then ask: *When is it appropriate to talk in this way? When is it inappropriate?* Have students work in pairs deciding which of the statements are examples of more formal speech and which exhibit informal speech. Then, considering each statement in turn, have students think of situations when a given statement would be appropriate or inappropriate.

b
- With books closed, ask students what a cover letter is. Elicit ideas about why an application form should be accompanied by a cover letter and ask for suggestions about the content of a cover letter. Also, discuss the fact that cover letters are written in a formal register and ask students to say why this is so.
- Ask students to open their books and to read through the short texts. Elicit or clarify that these sentences come from two cover letters. Have students work alone reading the cover letter excerpts and labeling each one *formal* or *informal* according to the register that the writer used.

c
- Organize students into pairs and have them compare and discuss their answers to the previous exercise.
- Check answers with the whole class and then ask students to make notes about the features (vocabulary, grammatical structures, tone) that make the informal excerpts inappropriate for a cover letter.
- To finish this section, write some of the informal sentences from the mixed up cover letters on the board and invite individual students to come to the front and to rewrite the sentences in a more formal, more appropriate register. Encourage other students to comment on the changes.

> **Answers**
> 1. informal 2. formal 3. formal 4. informal 5. informal 6. formal 7. formal 8. informal

d
- With books closed, remind students about the excerpts from the cover letters on the previous page. Focus their attention in particular on the excerpts that were written in a formal register. Now see if students can remember anything about the content of those excerpts. If they are stuck for ideas, read aloud the formal register excerpts from the text. Elicit ideas about what information should be included in a cover letter.
- Tell students that so far they have looked at the degree of formality a cover letter should exhibit and what information it should contain. Now explain that a third — and very important — characteristic of a good cover letter is the clarity with which it is written. Point out that an employer is unlikely to call a candidate whose cover letter is confusing and difficult to read for an interview even if that candidate's resume is very good. Explain to students that the following exercise focuses on words called connectors, which are the linking words which give a piece of writing cohesiveness and clarity.

Unit 1

- Ask students to open their books and to read the four sentences. Point out that each of the underlined words performs a very important function in its sentence, a function that adds meaning and clarity. Read aloud the first sentence and have students say what function the underlined word performs. Then have students work alone or in pairs completing the rest of the exercise. Check answers.

> **Answers**
> 1. offer additional information 2. show a time relationship 3. contrast two ideas 4. provide a reason

- With books closed, discuss the phenomenal growth and development of e-mail over the last few years. Ask students about their own e-mail use. Ask them what they use e-mail for, how often they send and receive e-mails, etc. Ask also about the register that they adopt when writing e-mails. Is it formal or informal?
- Discuss the fact that many transactions that formerly involved paper documents that had to be sent through the traditional postal service are now carried out electronically. Elicit examples. Also, elicit or point out that many companies now place job advertisements online and applicants can fill out online application forms or apply for jobs via e-mail.
- Tell students that they are going to listen to a teacher giving some advice on e-mail etiquette (etiquette = the formal rules of social behavior). Ask students to listen to the audio once through for the general idea.
- Then ask students to open their books and to read the sentences. Have them listen again and mark each sentence as a *Do* or a *Don't*. Check answers. Encourage students to comment on what they heard and to add any other rules about e-mail etiquette.

> **Answers**
> 1. Don't 2. Don't 3. Do 4. Do 5. Don't 6. Don't 7. Do

- Direct students' attention to the e-mail. Have them read through it briefly and then ask questions to check students' understanding.
- Ask students to work alone drafting an e-mail reply to Roger Davis' e-mail. Remind students that their e-mail should be written in a formal register and that it should follow the rules of e-mail etiquette.
- Then have students work in pairs reading through each other's work suggesting corrections, additions, deletions, and any other improvements. To end, ask individual students to read their e-mails aloud. Invite comment and discussion.

Additional Activity Unit 1 - Lesson 5   page 74

Answers
1. Answers will vary.
2. Answers will vary.

Writing Resource 1B   page 98

This writing task involves writing a cover letter to accompany a job application. Students have to arrange information in a logical sequence and consider matters of appropriate register and use of language.

Lesson 6 Time for the interview

SB Pages 12–13

The last lesson of this unit focuses on job interviews. After an introductory discussion activity, students study key collocations with the verbs *make* and *do*. The first listening activity deals with advice for interviewees and students. Then there is a focus on typical interview questions, which leads into oral practice. A second listening in which students evaluate both interviewers and interviewees is followed by a role play.

a
- With books closed, begin by sharing true anecdotes about people's experiences in interviews—interviews that went well, interviews that went badly, surprising questions that interviewers asked, embarrassing misunderstandings, etc. Encourage students to contribute to the discussion with anecdotes about people they know.
- Ask students to open their books and to read the discussion questions. Organize students into pairs and have them discuss the questions. Then open up the discussion for the whole class.

b
- Ask students to translate the verbs *make* and *do* into their own language. Elicit or point out that, since, in many languages, both of these verbs are translated by one single verb, learners of English often have trouble knowing which one to use. Explain that, although these two verbs mean generally the same thing, there are many fixed expressions where the verbs *make* and *do* are not interchangeable.
- Have students look at the expressions in the box. Read aloud the first item and ask: *What do we say in English—"do progress" or "make progress"?* Then have students work alone or in pairs combining the words and phrases with either *make* or *do* and writing sample phrases in their notebooks. Check answers.

> **Answers**
> make progress, make a good impression, make a profit, make money, make someone feel nervous
> do a course, do a job, do an exercise, do a favor, do business, do your best, do your homework

c
- Read aloud the first item and elicit first the correct verb *(make)* and then the correct form of the verb *(had made)*.
- Then ask students to work alone or in pairs completing the rest of the exercise. Check answers and at this point deal with any queries that students might have regarding vocabulary.

> **Answers**
> 1. had made 2. did 3. to make 4. doing 5. to make 6. doing

d
- With books closed, refer back to the discussion about interviews at the start of the lesson. Elicit stories and anecdotes about mistakes that people made at interviews. These might involve wearing the wrong clothes or saying the wrong thing, for example.
- Tell students that they are going to listen to a person giving some advice about how to perform well and give a good impression at an interview. Ask students to say what topics they think they will hear about. Then play the audio through once for students to get the general idea.
- Then ask students to open their books and to look at the points in the chart. Make sure that students understand that some of these items are things that an interviewee should do and some are things that he/she should not do. Have students listen to the audio again and check the appropriate boxes in the chart. Check answers.

> **Answers**
> 1. Do 2. Don't 3. Do 4. Do 5. Don't 6. Don't 7. Do 8. Don't

12 Unit 1

e
- With books closed, review the sort of topics that interviewers typically ask questions about. Elicit suggestion and write some ideas on the board.
- Ask students to open their books and to look briefly at the conversation. Elicit or clarify that it is the transcript of an interview and that it consists of just the interviewee's answers. Ask students to skim through these answers and to try to determine what sort of job the candidate has applied for.
- Then have students work alone or in pairs reading the answers carefully in order to reconstruct the questions that they think the interviewer asked. Check answers, pointing out that the answers given here are possible answers. Allow for slight variations.

> **Answers**
> 1. When did you graduate from college? 2. Have you had any work experience? 3. What appeals to you about working in our company? 4. What are your particular strengths? 5. What are your future plans? 6. What are your particular language and computer skills? 7. What do you see as your weaknesses?

f
- Organize students into pairs and have them read through the candidate's answers once more. Encourage them to think about how they would have answered these questions. Invite students to suggest improvements to any or all of the interviewee's answers.
- Open up the discussion for the whole class. Ask students to back up their opinions with reasoned arguments.

g
- Arrange students into new pairs and have them practice the interview incorporating any modifications that they have made to the interviewee's answers. Make sure that both students in each pair practice both of the roles in the interview. Then invite pairs of students to present the interview for the rest of the group.
- As extension, invite students to modify the interviewer's questions so that they are more demanding or more difficult to answer. Also, invite students to role-play interviews in which the interviewer has a stern and forbidding manner.

h (CD T-9)
- With books closed, discuss with students how one good way to improve one's interview technique is by observing or listening to other people in interviews. Ask students to listen to the three interviews in the audio once through for the general idea.
- Ask students to open their books and to read the questions so that they know what specific points they are to listen for. Play the audio again, this time pausing after each interview to give students time to write brief comments about the performances of both the interviewee and the interviewer.
- Have students compare and discuss their ideas in pairs or in small groups before opening up the discussion for the whole class.

i
- Ask students to select an interviewee who, in their opinion, did not give a good impression at the interview. Have students summarize in two or three sentences the things that this interviewee did wrong.
- Arrange students into pairs and have them role-play a conversation in which one student is this same interviewee and the other plays the part of a friend or counselor offering advice about how to improve their interview technique. Invite pairs of students to present their role plays for the rest of the group.

Lesson 6

Additional Activity Unit 1 - Lesson 6   page 74

Answers
1. 1. do 2. make 3. make 4. do 5. make 6. do 7. made 8. doing
2. Answers will vary.

Reading Resource 1B   page 88

Students read and complete an article about the role(s) of the Human Resources Department in a company. They summarize the main ideas of the article and complete a vocabulary task.

Answers
1. 1. traditional 2. material 3. firing 4. managers 5. fashion 6. maximize 7. objectives
    8. contact 9. asset 10. prosper
2. 1. simultaneously 2. precious 3. traditional 4. crucial 5. fair 6. prosper
3. Answers will vary.

Team Project 1

Prepare a recruitment dossier SB Page 14

- Organize students into groups of four or five. Read aloud the instructions and make sure that students understand what they are to do.
- Make clear that the finished product of this team project is not just a collection of documents, but a coherent dossier that covers all of the items listed in the instructions: background information about their chosen company, information about the Human Resources department of the company, recent job advertisements, information about the hiring process, information about selection procedures and short-listing, etc.
- Encourage students to package and illustrate their dossiers using a variety of visual media.

Review 1   SB page 72

Answer Key

A (Suggested answers.)
1. Good morning, Mrs. Madison. How are you? Could we speak to you for a few minutes? 2. What do you want to talk about? I'm in rather a hurry as I'm just about to leave. 3. Well, we're having some difficulty because we don't know how to find a summer job. We were wondering if you could give us some ideas. 4. I'm sorry but now is not really a good time for me to discuss this. Have you checked newspaper advertisements or talked to your family about available jobs? 5. Well, we thought that, being the school counselor, you would be the best person to talk to. 6. I see. Well, I think you should also try to help yourselves. Come for an interview tomorrow at 10. a.m. and please be punctual. 7. We will. Thank you, Mrs. Madison. See you tomorrow. Goodbye.

B
1. 1. c 2. d 3. a 4. e 5. b

C
1. Can you swim? 2. Does John have to attend the meeting this evening? 3. Will Magda drop by on her way home from work? 4. Did she use to visit? 5. Do you think she will do well in the exam?

Team Project 1 / Review 1

Unit 2

Selling is what it's all about you

Objectives

Language skills: discussing and evaluating ideas, reading for the general idea, understanding implied ideas, listening for specific information, using formal and informal registers, writing descriptions, identifying speakers in a conversation, interpreting graphs and charts, reading for specific information, describing statistical trends, giving oral presentations, using small talk and telephone language, writing memos, listening and taking notes, listening for attitude, writing letters, understanding vocabulary from context

Functions: expressing opinions, expressing tendencies, marking contrasts, persuading, complaining

Grammar: phrasal verbs, real conditionals in the present or in the future, word formation, passive voice, indirect questions, present perfect

Lesson 1 Have you got what it takes?   SB Pages 16–17

In this lesson, students consider the aptitudes and personal qualities that make someone a good salesperson. They begin with discussion activities and a reading that invites them to assess their suitability for the world of sales. Students then practice describing people using language for describing tendencies. After a listening activity, students complete activities about register and about phrasal verbs before finishing with a writing task.

a
- With books closed, ask students if they know anyone who works in the field of sales. Invite students to share what they know about sales, the work of a salesperson, the challenges and rewards of working in sales, etc. Discuss people's received ideas about salespeople derived from portrayals in movies, novels, TV shows, and ask students how this image compares with real life.
- Ask students to open their books and to read the statements. Then organize students into pairs or small groups and have them discuss the questions. Finally open up the discussion for the whole group, focusing on the statements that provoked the most interesting reactions or differences of opinion.

b
- By way of a quick show of hands, find out how many students in the class consider themselves capable of working in sales or how many have considered this field. Discuss the idea that sales is not an area of business that appeals to everyone and the idea that not everyone is cut out for a career in sales.
- Ask students to read the instructions. Then elicit a few initial ideas and write them on the board. Show students that these qualities can be expressed in various ways. For example, we can write a list of adjectives (*determined, ambitious,* etc.) or a quality can be expressed as an abstract noun (*determination, ambition,* etc.)
- Have students work alone compiling their lists of ideas. Then ask students to talk in pairs, comparing and discussing their ideas. Invite individual students to share their ideas with the rest of the group. Encourage comment and debate.

c
- With books closed, initiate a discussion on the subject of personality. Invite students to share information about, for example, two members of their family who have contrasting personalities or the way in which two people can be good friends though they do not necessarily share the same character traits.
- Ask students to open their books and to skim through the text briefly for the general idea. Then ask students to read the text again and use it to evaluate their own personalities. Then have students compare and discuss their ideas in pairs.

d
- Direct students' attention to the expressions in the box. Ask students to read through the text once more looking for examples of phrases that express a tendency and phrases that are used to mark a contrast.
- Check answers.

> **Answers**
> **Tendency:** tends to be, may be, show a tendency, generally like, can be, are likely to be, have a tendency to be
> **Contrast:** though, while, on the other hand

e
- Review the language highlighted in the previous exercise. Point out the way expressions for describing a tendency and phrases that express contrast are particularly useful when talking about someone's personality since most people are not 100% one thing or another all the time. Instead, people display various shades of a particular quality. Furthermore, within the same person, we can often observe character traits that show marked contrasts.
- Ask students to look at the instructions. Read aloud the example. Then have students work alone or in pairs completing the exercise. Check answers.

> **Answers**
> Though Robert can sometimes be aggressive, at other times he can be very pleasant. Though Chris generally likes a good time, while working he is capable of achieving a lot. While Naomi is generally very compassionate, she can be very decisive and persistent. Though Mark has a tendency to be careless sometimes, he is usually accurate and precise.

f
CD T-10
- With books closed, refer students back to **b** where they discussed the qualities that they think make a good salesperson. Then have students listen to the audio once through for the general idea.
- Ask students to open their books and to read through the points in the list. Have them listen again and number the points in the order that they are mentioned.

> **Answers**
> 5, 1, 4, 2, 6, 3

g
- Read aloud the four expressions. Clarify that they are all informal expressions. Ask students to work in pairs rewriting each expression in a more formal, less idiomatic way.

> **Answers**
> 1. preventing someone from shutting the door 2. forcing someone to let you into their house
> 3. deceiving or cheating the person 4. paying unwillingly for a product

h
- Read aloud the phrasal verbs. Reiterate that in almost every instance, phrasal verbs—common in conversational English—can be substituted with more formal, single-word equivalents.
- Have students work in pairs finding one-word verbs that mean the same as the phrasal verbs. If it helps students, play the audio one more time so that they can hear the phrasal verbs in context. Check answers.

> **Answers**
> 1. produce 2. notice 3. use 4. understand

i
- Briefly summarize all the information that students have seen in this lesson. Then ask students to write some notes and then a first draft of a description of what, in their opinion, makes a good salesperson.
- Encourage students to read each other's work and to offer suggestions for improvements before they write out a final version. Invite individual students to read their descriptions for the rest of the group.

Additional Activity Unit 2 - Lesson 1 — page 75

Answers
1 1. features 2. benefits 3. prospect 4. money hours 5. buying signal 6. close
2 Answers will vary.

Lesson 2   Have you got what it takes?   SB Pages 18–19

This lesson focuses students' attention more closely on specific sales situations. They explore the dynamics of sales transactions—how salespeople behave and how customers react to them. A discussion activity is followed by work on the contexts of sales conversations. Students then do a role play before completing a series of activities based around a telephone conversation. The grammatical focus of the lesson is real conditionals in the present or in the future. To end the lesson, students practice writing conditional sentences.

a
- With books closed, have the class brainstorm a list of all the ways that it is possible nowadays to make a purchase of some kind. The list might include traditional store purchases, mail order, online shopping, informal purchases from friends, door-to-door sales, etc. Write students' ideas on the board.
- Ask students to open their books and have them read and then discuss the questions in pairs. Then open up the discussion for the whole class.

b
- With books closed, elicit ideas about the sorts of questions that customers frequently ask of sales assistants in stores and the typical questions that salespeople ask of customers.
- Ask students to open their books and to read through the questions. Read aloud the first question and elicit the correct answer. Then have students work alone or in pairs matching the remaining questions with the correct responses. Also, have students discuss the places or situations where one might overhear exchanges like these. Check answers.

Answers
1. e 2. d 3. f 4. c 5. a 6. b

c
- Direct students' attention to the role play situations. Choose one situation and elicit examples of the sorts of questions that might be asked by either the sales assistant or by the customer in this situation.
- Organize students into pairs and have them work on their role plays. Then invite pairs of students to present their role plays for the rest of the group. Review the role plays and draw to students' attention the types of questions and responses that were used.

d
- With books closed, elicit examples of the sorts of goods or services that are commonly sold by telemarketing. Write some suggestions on the board. Ask students if they have ever received a call from a telemarketer and, if so, for what type of product. Elicit observation and comment on the growth of this type of selling in recent years.
- Ask students to open their books and to skim briefly through the extracts of the conversation. Elicit that one of the speakers is a telemarketer and that he/she is trying to sell the services of a telephone company. Ask students if telephone companies in their country use this method to sell their services.
- Read aloud the example. Then have students work alone or in pairs completing the remaining sentences with the verbs in the box.

Answers
1. speak 2. help 3. work 4. reduce 5. give 6. sign 7. make 8. check

Lesson 2

e
- Read aloud the first sentence from the previous exercise and clarify that this sentence is spoken by the salesperson.
- Then have students go through conversation extracts and sort them into the two categories, salesperson and prospective customer.

f (CD T-11)
- Before playing the audio, ask students if they think the salesperson succeeded in closing the sale with the prospective customer. Have them offer evidence to support their views.
- Ask students to listen to the conversation and to check their answers to the previous exercise.
- For an extension exercise, ask students to work in pairs preparing their own versions of the conversation. Emphasize that they do not have to reproduce the script word for word but rather arrive at an approximation.

> **Answers**
> **salesperson:** 1, 3, 6, 7, and 8
> **prospective customer:** 2, 4, and 5

g
- With books closed, clarify the concept of a condition. Talk about everyday situations that illustrate the idea of one action being conditional upon another. For example, mention activities that depend on favorable weather conditions or mention "deals" that people make in which one person agrees to do something for another but asks for something in exchange. Elicit or explain that the key word used to express such conditions is *if*.
- Ask students to open their books and to look at the information in the chart. Read aloud the first item from the Condition column and point out that a phrase like this cannot stand alone. Implicitly, there needs to be another clause to complete the meaning. Elicit the correct answer from the Action column.
- Then have students work alone or in pairs completing the rest of the exercise. Check answers. Elicit or point out that in these conditional sentences, the verb is in the simple present (either indicative or imperative) in both the *if* clause and the action clause. Tell students that this type of conditional is sometimes referred to as the zero conditional.

> **Answers**
> 1. c 2. d 3. b 4. a

h
- Read aloud the first item and elicit a conditional sentence. Point out how one possible answer *(If you want to save money, check the prices in different stores.)* uses a simple imperative or another possibility uses the modal verb should *(If you want to save money, you should check the prices in different stores.)*
- Then ask students to work alone or in pairs completing the rest of the exercise. Check answers. Have individual students write their sentences on the board. Make sure that students punctuate their conditional sentences properly with the comma in the correct place between the condition clause and the action clause.

> **Answers**
> 1. If you want to save money, (you should) check the prices in different stores. 2. If you are happy with our offer, (please / you can) sign the contract and send it back. 3. If you require a demonstration of our products, our salesman will be happy to do so. 4. If you shop online, you will (probably) save money. 5. If you want to contact someone quickly, send an e-mail.

Additional Activity Unit 2 - Lesson 2 — page 75

Answers
1. Answers will vary.
2. Answers will vary.

Lesson 3 Sales have increased by 20%   SB Pages 20-21

The focus of this lesson is the way statistical information, in this case about sales, can be presented in graphical form or in written form. After an initial discussion activity, students examine and interpret information in a bar chart. They then analyze sales information presented in a text. The lesson then shifts its focus to giving oral presentations, something that people in business are often called on to do. Students carry out a discussion task, two types of listening task and, finally, they prepare an oral presentation.

a
- With books closed, show students a number of samples of charts and graphs of different types (line graphs, bar charts, pie charts, etc.). These can be taken from magazines and newspapers, especially the financial and business sections, and they do not have to be related to sales figures. Elicit observation and comment about the way the information is presented.
- Ask students to open their books. Read aloud the discussion questions. Then organize students into pairs to discuss the questions. If possible, distribute photocopied samples of bar charts, pie charts, etc. for students to look at while they are discussing the questions.

b
- Ask students to look at the chart. Elicit that it is a bar chart. Also, ask students to say why they think it was decided to present the information in this format instead of as a pie chart. Draw to students' attention the fact that, by convention, data referring to time is always placed along the horizontal axis.
- Read aloud the first question and elicit the correct answer. Then have students work alone or in pairs answering the remaining questions. Check answers.

> **Answers**
> 1. The overall trend is upward. 2. It occurred between 1998 and 2001. 3. There was only a very slight increase.

c
- With books closed, elicit the names of large supermarket chains operating in the students' country. Ask students whether these supermarkets sell organic food of any kind (fruits, vegetables, organic milk, etc.). Ask students if any of the products that they or their families consume are labeled organic. Then elicit ideas and comments about the introduction and growth of organic food products in recent years.
- Ask students to open their books and to look at the text. Have them skim through it quickly for the general idea. If necessary, deal with any doubts students have regarding key vocabulary items. Then ask students to read the article again carefully and to answer the questions alone or in pairs. Check and discuss answers.

> **Answers**
> 1. It is responsible for Sainsbury's continued recovery. 2. Because of increased awareness of health issues and consumers' desire to know where food is coming from. 3. They have increased by 20%. 4. There has been a broadening of the socioeconomic group who buy organic food.

d
- Draw students' attention to the pairs of sample sentences. First, make sure that students understand that these sentences show two ways of saying the same thing. Elicit observations about both the forms of the words highlighted in bold type and about the order of the words within each sentence. Elicit that, in English, adjectives invariably come before the nouns that they describe and that adverbs often, though not always, come after the verbs that they modify.
- Ask students to work alone or in pairs completing the two tables with the correct adjectives, nouns, verbs, and adverbs. Have them add at least one more example of each combination of words. Check answers.

Lesson 3

> **Answers**
> **adjective noun:** steady decrease, sharp decline
> **verb adverb:** increased slightly, grew noticeably

- Read aloud the discussion questions. Organize students into pairs and have them discuss the questions.
- Then open up the discussion for the whole class. Elicit ideas regarding the types of information or the types of situation that lend themselves to oral presentations.

- With books closed, tell students that they are going to hear an expert offering advice about how to give an effective presentation in front of other people. Ask students to listen to the audio once through for the general idea.
- Then ask students to open their books and to look briefly at the list of DOs and DON'Ts. Have students listen again and mark each statement as a DO or a DON'T. Check answers. Then, ask students if they have any other pieces of advice or tips that they would add to the list.

CD T-12

> **Answers**
> Do: Select essential information, Come with notes in order, Organize content in a logical way, Use introduction to inform listeners, Establish good rapport with audience, Make eye contact, Bring talk to a proper conclusion
> Don't: Include all details, Include comments not related to the topic, Speak quickly and loudly

- Referring to the information in the previous exercise, discuss the idea that giving presentations is something that almost anyone can do, but that not everyone does well.
- Tell students that they are going to hear short extracts from three separate presentations. Have students listen the first time without taking any notes. Then ask them to listen again and to evaluate and write comments about each speaker. Discuss students' answers and elicit ideas regarding the advice that they would give to the speakers who they consider did not make very good presentations.

CD T-13

- Read aloud the instructions. Ask students to think of a particular industry or market that is relevant to their country. Then elicit ideas about the places where students might be able to find up-to-date and reliable information about sales in their chosen field.
- Give students some research time and then, in a subsequent session, ask individual students to give oral presentations summarizing recent movements and trends in a particular sector of the economy. Encourage students to use the type of language that they have been studying in this lesson and to use visual materials such as graphs and charts to illustrate their presentations.

Additional Activity Unit 1 - Lesson 4   **page 73**

Answers
1. Answers will vary.   2. Answers will vary.

Writing Resource 2A   **page 99**

In this task, students research and prepare a report describing recent sales trends and phenomena in a chosen sector of the market. Along with their findings, they present relevant graphical data.

Lesson 4 Dealing with the customer SB Pages 22–23

In this lesson, students look again at specific sales situations, in particular, placing an order for some goods over the telephone. Students listen to conversations to complete order forms and they also consider the sort of small talk that frequently takes place between people involved in sales and their regular customers. The language focus of this lesson is the passive voice, especially as used in transactions such as ordering, delivering, checking information, complaining, etc. Students also practice writing memos and discuss real-life cases of customer dissatisfaction.

CD T-14

- With books closed, ask students to brainstorm and write lists of as many items of furniture as they can think of in two minutes. Then ask students to name items of furniture used in restaurants and hotels.
- Tell students that they are going to hear a conversation in which someone from a hotel places an order for some furniture. Ask students to listen to the audio once through for the general idea.
- Ask students to open their books and to look at the page of notes. Then have students listen to the audio again and complete the notes with the correct information. Check answers.

> **Answers**
> double beds 10, single beds 20, closets 30, dressers 30, Order needed by May 15th

CD T-15

- Ask students what they understand by the expression *small talk*. Elicit examples in the students' own language of expressions and phrases that are often used in small talk before people who know each other begin talking about other things.
- Ask students to listen again to the conversation from the previous exercise and to make notes of the phrases that the speakers use that could be categorized as small talk. Check and discuss students' ideas. Examples include, *It's been a while.* and *How is business?*

c
- Referring to the previous exercise, make clear the idea that small talk occurs more naturally between people who have had some previous contact. Point out, however, that some small talk topics (one obvious example is the weather) can be used in small talk from the very first occasion that two people meet.
- Ask students to look at the topics listed in the box and, working in pairs, have them discuss which topics would be suitable as small talk in a business conversation with a new customer. Check and discuss answers. Students will probably mention the weather and how happy the person is to take the order as the only two safe and acceptable topics of small talk. Discuss the other topics and have students say when, if at all, they would be acceptable as topics for small talk. Encourage students to explain their answers.

d
- Ask students to read the information on the role cards. Then, organize students into pairs and have them role-play conversations based on this situation. Encourage students to use the small talk that they consider appropriate for this situation.
- Invite pairs of students to present their role plays for the rest of the group. Invite comment and discussion.

CD T-16

- Tell students that they are going to hear another conversation in which someone places an order by telephone.
- Have them listen to the conversation and complete the order form with the correct information. If necessary, play the audio twice. Check answers.

Lesson 4

> **Answers**
> Company: Totally Natural, Delivery address: Riverside Way, Delham, Account number: 1979, Purchase Order: TF1979, Order: 10 kg of cauliflower, 20 kg of potatoes, 15 kg of onions, Transportation: truck

f
- With books closed, but referring to the merchandise that was featured in the conversations that students heard in previous exercises, elicit ideas about the sorts of problems that could occur with these orders—problems that would cause inconvenience to the customer. Students may come up with ideas such as deliveries that do not match what was ordered in quantity, size, color, etc., merchandise that arrives late, merchandise that arrives damaged, etc.
- Ask students to open their books and to look at the first item in the exercise. Read aloud the first answer and tell students that this is an example of the passive voice. Then convert the sentence to the active voice, i.e. *We sent out the laptops ten days ago.* Elicit ideas about the difference between the two sentences, both in terms of the grammar and also in terms of the effect that each sentence has. Elicit or point out that people often use passive voice sentences because they sound less personal and, in certain business situations, this might be very useful.
- Ask students to work alone or in pairs completing the rest of the exercise. Check answers and spend some time examining the various tenses that can be used with the passive voice.

> **Answers**
> 1. The laptops were sent out ten days ago.   2. Your software is being dispatched by our staff as we speak.   3. Those DVDs are expected today. They should be shipped to you by Friday.

g
- Review the idea that the passive voice is often used in situations where the person or thing performing an action is not as important as the action itself or it is not known or it is implicitly understood by everyone. Add that the passive voice is also used when it is more convenient not to mention a subject by name.
- Ask students to read the information in the note. Point out that we may not know who exactly sent out the order. All that is known is that the order was sent out. Then have students write a short memo asking a colleague to trace an online order that has not been delivered.

h
- Discuss briefly the idea that consumers have rights that are protected by law and elicit some examples of these from the students' country. Read aloud the first problem from the box and ask students to identify which of the four consumer rights this corresponds to.
- Then have students work alone or in pairs completing the rest of the exercise.

> **Answers**
> 1. c   2. d   3. a   4. b

i
- Organize students into pairs and have them share real-life anecdotes about times when they experienced a problem as a consumer.
- Open up the discussion for the whole class. Encourage students to comment and debate.

 Additional Activity Unit 2 - Lesson 4   page 76

Answers
1. 1. to   2. through   3. by   4. over   5. on   **2.** Answers will vary.

Lesson 5 Dealing with complaints   SB Pages 24–25

This lesson picks up the topic of complaints from the end of the previous lesson and gives students more practice, especially in writing a letter of complaint. After a discussion activity, students listen and take notes about customers' complaints. They then work on role plays in which they practice using indirect questions. The next listening activity focuses on the attitudes and behavior of customers and salespeople when dealing with a problem. In the last part of the lesson, students study the parts of a formal letter before writing a reply.

a
- Ask students to read the discussion questions. Organize students into pairs and have them discuss the questions.
- Then ask students to form groups of four and to share their ideas and anecdotes in their group.
- Finally, open up the discussion for the whole group. Discuss general ideas regarding complaints. Ask, for example: *In this country, do people tend to complain a lot about goods and services? Do people obtain results by complaining?*

b CD T-17
- Read aloud the instructions. Check that students understand the meaning of *refund*. Elicit anecdotes about situations where a person claimed a refund on something he / she had bought but did not obtain one.
- Play the audio once through for students to get the general idea. Then play the track again and have students take brief notes about why each person is claiming a refund. Check answers.
- Arrange students in pairs and have them discuss whether they think each person they heard should receive a refund. When discussing students' ideas, have them explain their reasons.

> **Answers**
> Customer 1: doesn't like the color of a jacket
> Customer 2: zoom lens of the camera doesn't work
> Customer 3: fuzzy picture on TV because customer dropped it

c
- Direct students' attention to the expressions in the box. Ask students to say what they observe about these expressions. Elicit or explain that, *I would like...* is a more polite way of saying, *I want...* and that openings like *I was wondering if...* and *Do you think...* are also polite variations on blunter, more direct questions that could, in certain circumstances, sound abrupt or rude. Point out that it is very common for people to use expressions like these in formal situations. Elicit similar phrases in the students' own language.
- Ask students to read the role play situations carefully. Then organize students into pairs and have them prepare role plays based on any two of the situations. Encourage them to use the expressions from the box.
- Invite pairs of students to present their role plays for the rest of the group.

d
- Organize students into pairs or small groups and ask them to discuss the rights (if any) of the consumer in each of the role play situations from the previous exercise, whether they selected the situations from their own role play or not.
- Then open up the discussion for the whole class, focusing on the situations that proved to be more controversial or about which there was the most disagreement.

e CD T-18
- Remind students of the topics they discussed at the start of this lesson, in particular regarding their experiences when trying to make a complaint about something. Tell students that they are going to listen to three different situations in which people complain. Have them listen to the first part of the audio and then elicit reactions. Ask: *How does the customer feel? How does the salesperson react? Is the problem resolved or just postponed?* Invite comment about how the two people handled the situation.

- Then ask students to listen to the other two conversations and to take notes about the same points that they considered for the first situation. Again, invite observation and comment. Encourage students to imagine themselves in the role of either the customer or the salesperson in each case and to imagine how they would feel and how they would react in such a situation.

f
- With books closed, hold up in front of the class examples of formal, business letters. It does not matter if students cannot read any of the words but try to make sure that they can see the general layout of the letters, that is, the address, the date, the greeting, the signature, etc. (If necessary, make enlarged photocopies of the letters so that students can see the layout more clearly.) Elicit observation and comment. Draw to student's attention the orderly, neat effect that is created by a letter that is laid out well.
- Ask students to open their books and to look at the letter. Then have them look at the items in the box. Explain that these are some of the essential elements in a formal letter of complaint. Have students write the number of each item in the correct place at the right-hand side of the letter. Check answers.

> **Answers**
> In order from top to bottom: 7. customer address, 6. date, 4. salutation, 5. purpose of letter, 3. proof of purchase, 8. problem, 1. desired outcome, 2. signature

g
- Ask students to imagine that they work for Super Electrical Stores in the Customer Service department. Have them read the instructions carefully before drafting a reply to Jerome Calvin. Encourage students to work in pairs reading each other's work and making corrections and offering suggestions for improvements.
- Then ask students to write out a final, corrected version of their letter, paying careful attention to the layout and the general look of the letter. Invite individual students to read their letters aloud.

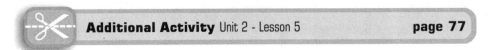

Additional Activity Unit 2 - Lesson 5 — page 77

Answers
1. 1. Include 2. Type 3. Keep 4. State 5. Send 6. Avoid 7. Save   **2.** Answers will vary.

Reading Resource 2A — page 89

This reading deals with recent examples of product boycotts from around the world. Students complete various comprehension tasks. Language work focuses on words and phrases for expressing relationships of cause and effect.

Answers
Answers will vary, but may include the following:
A Target: Nestlé / Reasons for boycott: marketing of powdered baby milk in less developed countries
Target: Esso (ExxonMobil) / Reasons for boycott: policies and actions that harm the environment
Target: Jyllands-Posten newspaper / Reasons for boycott: publishing cartoons that were offensive to many Muslims
B 1. True 2. False 3. True 4. True 5. False   **C** Answers will vary.

Writing Resource 2B — page 100

This task involves writing a formal letter of complaint about a product or service that proved unsatisfactory. Students state the problem and provide relevant details and make clear what action they expect to be taken.

Lesson 6 Buying and selling on the Internet   SB Pages 26–27

This lesson focuses on the most recent trend in retail sales—online shopping. After a brief discussion activity, students read about a fictitious company (based on Amazon.com) that has been very successful selling books and various other products over the Internet. They then complete reading comprehension and vocabulary exercises. The grammar focus of this lesson is the present perfect for describing actions that began in the past and that continue in the present. Students then complete a listening task and take notes. Discussion and speaking activities round off the lesson.

a
- With books closed, elicit the names of the principal companies that provide Internet access in the students' country. Ask also for the names of well-known Web sites where people can buy things. These may include the Web sites of existing companies or sites that were specially created for the Internet.
- Ask students to open their books and to read the discussion questions. Then organize students into pairs and have them discuss the questions.

b
- Ask students to look just at the photograph. *Ask: Who do you think this man is? What does he do for a living?* Have students skim through the text quickly to get the gist of its content.
- Have students read the questions at the foot of the page. Then ask them to read the text again carefully and, working alone, to answer the questions. Have students compare and discuss their answers in pairs before checking the answers with the whole group.

> **Answers**
> 1. Because of its phenomenal growth. 2. Because of the large pool of technical know-how that is there. 3. The company is customer-centered and it meets the various needs of the customer. 4. Through having a quick turnaround.

c
- Read aloud the first item in the exercise and ask students to find a word in the first paragraph of the text about Mike Gore that means the same or nearly the same as this word.
- Then have students work alone or in pairs completing the rest of the exercise. Check answers and then deal with any other queries students may have regarding vocabulary items.

> **Answers**
> 1. phenomenal 2. generated 3. broad range 4. distinctive 5. alerted

d
- Ask students to read through the text about Booksandstuff and to find examples of verbs in the present perfect. Have them underline the sentences where these verbs are found. Then, write on the board one of the present perfect sentences, for example, *Booksandstuff's customer base has grown to well over 30 million.* Then ask: *When did this growth start?* to elicit the fact that it started at some time in the past. Then ask: *Is there still growth now? Will there be more growth in the future?* Explain that because, as far as we know, this is true, we use the present perfect to describe the action rather than the simple past, the use of which would imply that the growth was something that happened and that is now over.
- Read aloud the first item in the exercise and elicit a complete sentence using the present perfect. Then have students work alone or in pairs completing the rest of the exercise. Check answers. Discuss those cases where either the present perfect simple or the present perfect progressive are acceptable forms.

Lesson 6   27

Answers
1. Sophie has shopped/has been shopping online for several years now. 2. Daniel worked in Singapore until 1999 and he has been working/has worked in Japan since then. 3. Online travel booking has changed the face of air travel. 4. In the past, tourists took package holidays, but independent travel has increased in recent years. 5. Booksandstuff.com did not show a large profit up to 2002, but since that year profits have shot up.

CD T-19

- Tell students that they are going to listen to someone giving some advice and some warnings about online shopping. Before playing the audio, elicit some ideas about the sort of things that students expect to hear. Then ask students to look at the headings in the notes so that know what to listen for.
- Ask students to listen to the audio and to take brief notes. If necessary, let students hear the audio twice. Check answers.

Answers
Before you buy: do research on company, check all contact details, consider all costs, read terms and conditions of sale
How to pay: with a credit card
Precautions: look for 's' for 'secure' sign at the bottom, keep copies of receipts and acknowledgements
Where to go for help: consumer affairs office

f
- Discuss briefly the phenomenal development and growth of e-commerce. Remind students, especially younger students, that the commercial potential of the World Wide Web only started to become a reality in the mid 1990s. Invite students to share their experiences, opinions, anecdotes, etc. related to the world of online commerce.
- Have students read the steps for setting up an online store. Then organize students into pairs or small groups and have them decide on a logical sequence. Elicit answers, which may well vary from group to group. Discuss these differences as a whole class.

g
- Remind students of what they learned in Lesson 3 about giving oral presentations. Have them read the instructions carefully.
- Then ask students to work in pairs preparing presentations that explain how online shopping works and discuss the pros and cons (the advantages and disadvantages) of online shopping. Encourage students to include in their presentation some activity that invites their audience to participate, to comment on the topic, etc.

Additional Activity Unit 2 - Lesson 6   **page 77**

Answers
1. Answers will vary.   **2.** Answers will vary.

Reading Resource 2B   **page 90**

Students read an article about consumer protection agencies and complete a variety of reading comprehension tasks. They then write notes summarizing the information they read.

Answers
A Answers will vary.
B 1. Consumerism, consumer issues 2. The products that are the most controlled 3. Product labels and packaging 4. There have been cases of advertising 5. Questionable selling practices
C True sentences: 1, 3, and 4

Unit 2

Team Project 2

Prepare a consumer report

SB Page 28

- Organize students into groups of four or five. Read aloud the instructions and make sure that students understand what they are to do.
- Ask students if there are consumer magazines in their country and what sort of consumer reports they contain. Ask students if they or any members of their families ever consult consumer magazines to research products before deciding which one to buy.
- Have students prepare their reports. Encourage them to use a variety of visual media (photographs, diagrams, charts, tables, graphs, etc.) to present their findings.

Review 2

SB page 73

Answer Key

A

1. e 2. a 3. b 4. f 5. c 6. d

1. Many Internet companies were set up but / though not all of them were successful.
2. People let shops know when they are unhappy with a product but / though they rarely return to say they are happy with a product.
3. A letter or phone call gives limited information about a candidate while / whereas an interview allows the employer to meet the interviewee face to face.
4. Both products were launched at the same time but / though the performance of both has been quite different.
5. Work in the future will be quite different from what it is at the present but / though it is unlikely that it will be any less stressful than it is at the moment.
6. We cannot normally choose when to receive a phone call while / whereas we can usually choose when to read an e-mail.

B

1. The event turned out to be a great success. 2. Online communication with customers picks up on the problems they were experiencing. 3. The new employee tuned into what the department expected of him. 4. The company needs to build on previous marketing strategies.

C

1. If you want to succeed in your career, you must work hard. 2. If a businessman sets up a new business, he has to give it a catchy name. 3. If world trade and globalization generate confidence, they observe responsible business practices. 4. If the student uses his credit card carefully, he doesn't run up a lot of debt. 5. If the marketing department is successful, it understands the target market.

Unit 3

Marketing the product

Objectives

Language skills: discussing and evaluating ideas, listening and taking notes, describing products, listening for the general idea, writing definitions, word formation, writing descriptions, preparing questionnaires, reading for the general idea, understanding vocabulary from context, using formal and informal registers, skimming, identifying speakers in a conversation, writing e-mails, connecting ideas

Functions: expressing opinions, persuading, making comparisons, making requests, expressing cause and effect

Grammar: passive voice (present), compound adjectives, comparative adjectives, present perfect contrasted with past simple, multiword verbs, linking words

Lesson 1 Telling the world about your product   SB Pages 30–31

In this lesson, students look at advertising. They discuss and analyze some printed advertisements and consider the techniques that advertisers employ to make their advertising effective. Listening material focuses on various types of advertising while the language focus for this lesson is the use of the passive voice in the present for describing processes, techniques, etc. To end the lesson, students work in groups preparing advertisements and then trying them out on their classmates.

a
- With books closed, show students photographs or write on the board the names of places in their country or in other countries that are well known for displaying a great concentration of advertisements in a relatively small space. Well-known examples might include Times Square in New York City and Piccadilly Circus in London. Elicit observation and comment about these places and have students try to describe what these places are like, especially when lit up at night.
- Ask students to open their books and have them read the discussion questions. Organize students into pairs and have them discuss the questions. Then open up the discussion for the whole group.

b
- Ask students to look at the advertisements. Elicit the meaning of some of the abbreviations used in the ads, for example, *in.* for *inch* and *yr.* for *year*.
- Draw students' attention to the list of features and characteristics below the ads. Then have students work alone or in pairs identifying phrases from the ads that fit these categories. Check answers, which may vary from student to student.

> **Answers**
> choice: range of models
> after-sales service/protection: 1-yr. mfg. warranty, 3-yr. warranty
> quality: faster processor
> appealing features: lightweight, 14-in screen
> price/cost: 10% off, Today only $810, from 20% off, an additional 15% off sales price

c
- Read the questions aloud. Organize students into pairs and have them discuss the questions. Then open up the discussion for the whole class. Ask students to say where they might expect to find ads in this format (magazines, newspapers, leaflets, etc.) and have them discuss how the advertisers of these products would advertise in other media, for example, TV, billboards in the street, on the Internet, etc.

d
- Direct students' attention to the phrases in the box. Model them by describing recent real-life advertisements that have appeared on TV or on billboards.
- Arrange students into pairs and have them discuss current advertisements - in any medium - that have caught their attention recently. Then, as a whole class, invite pairs of students to describe (or even act out) their chosen ads and to explain what it is that they like about them.

- Read aloud the categories in the first column of the chart. Tell students that they are going to hear someone talking about different types of advertising. Make clear that this does not refer to different advertising media (newspapers, radio, TV, etc.) but to the intentions and strategy of the advertiser.
- Ask students to listen to the talk once through for the general idea. Then have them listen again and complete the chart with brief notes. Check and discuss answers.

> **Answers**
> informative: factual information about prices, special offers, etc. usually about household products
> persuasive: beneficial changes products bring to ones' life, often used for beauty products, cosmetic surgery
> competitive: claims that a company's products or services are better than those of the competition, used with many types of product or service

- From the tapescript for the listening material, read aloud examples of the passive voice in the present tense. Review the fact that the passive voice is often used to describe processes or techniques where what happens is more important or more relevant than the agent of the action, or when the agent is not known, or it is implicitly understood by everyone. Read aloud the first sentence of the text.
- Then have students work alone or in pairs completing the rest of the text with the correct passive voice form of the given verbs. Check answers.

> **Answers**
> 1. is used 2. are persuaded 3. are convinced 4. are made 5. is purchased 6. is needed

- Briefly, as a whole class, brainstorm ideas regarding the different media that can be used for advertising and discuss the relative merits, advantages, efficiency, impact, etc. of each type.
- Arrange students into pairs and have them discuss ideas for an advertisement. Remind students to focus clearly on their intended market and on the type of medium that is the best vehicle for their ad.

- Read aloud the phrases and expressions in the box. Review and discuss the idea that all advertising attempts to influence the potential customer and persuade him / her into becoming a real customer.
- Invite pairs of students to present their ads for the rest of the group. Invite observation and comment. As an alternative option, ask students to imagine that they all work for the same advertising agency. When students present their proposals, the rest of the class takes on the role of advertising executives whose job it is to choose the most effective ad.

 Additional Activity Unit 3 - Lesson 1   page 78

Answers
1. 6, 4, 1, 5, 3, 8, 2, 7
2. Answers will vary.
3. Answers will vary.

Lesson 2 Brands

SB Pages 32–33

The initial focus of this lesson is the topic of brands, logos, and trademarks — terms with meanings that sometimes overlap. Students start the lesson with some discussion activities and then listen to a talk on the subject of branding. They then complete some vocabulary and word formation exercises and, in particular, study hyphenated compound adjectives from the world of marketing. Grammar work focuses on comparative forms and, to end the lesson, students write descriptions of well-known brands.

a
- With books closed, show students a selection of ads cut from magazines or newspapers. Try to include some ads for products made by companies that are so well known that their logo or trademark has greater prominence than the name of the company itself. Invite observation and comment.
- Ask students to open their books and to read the questions. Then organize students into pairs and have them discuss the questions. Then open up the discussion for the whole group. At this point, it may well be necessary to clarify definitions of these terms (see below) while, at the same time, pointing out that these terms are sometimes used almost interchangeably. One very simple way of defining the terms is that a logo is one part of a trademark and a trademark is one element in a brand.

> **Vocabulary Note:**
> *brand* = A collection of images and ideas representing the product(s) of a single company or manufacturer. A brand is both the symbolic representation of information connected to a company, and its products / services. This includes concrete symbols such as a name, logo, fonts, design and color schemes, symbols, and sound.
> *trademark* = A distinctive sign legally reserved and used by an organization to identify itself and its products / services and to distinguish itself (and its products / services) from others. A trademark can comprise a name, word, phrase, logo, symbol, design, image, or a combination of these elements.
> *logo* = A graphical identifying element, symbol, or icon of a trademark or a brand, often used along with its logotype, words or phrases set in a unique typeface or arranged in a particular way.

b
- Draw students' attention to the selection of images. Read aloud the questions. Then have students work in pairs answering the questions.
- Then open up the discussion for the whole group.

c
- With books closed, tell students that they are going to hear a talk on the subject of brands and branding. Play the audio once through for students to get the general idea.
- Ask students to open their books and to read through the statements so that they have an idea of what to listen for. Play the audio again and have students mark the statements that are true according to what they heard. Check answers.

> **Answers**
> True statements: 2 3 5 6

d
- Read aloud the first item. Make sure that students understand that the information in this exercise comes from the listening material in the previous activity.
- Have students work alone or in pairs completing the rest of the exercise. Check and discuss answers.

> **Answers**
> 1. d 2. a 3. b 4. e 5. c

e
- Choose one of the expressions from the box and write it on the board. As a whole class activity, elicit a definition of the term as it is used in marketing. As students add suggestions, modify and perfect the definition until it is as complete and as precise as possible.
- Organize students into small groups and have them discuss and write definitions of each of the terms. Tell them that they may use dictionaries but point out that their dictionaries will provide general definitions rather than definitions from the world of marketing. Check and discuss answers.

f
- Read aloud the first item and point out how the adjective *revolutionary* is derived from the noun *revolution*.
- Then have students work alone or in pairs completing the rest of the exercise. Check answers and elicit other, similar pairs of nouns and adjectives that change in the same way.

> **Answers**
> 1. revolution 2. reliability 3. sophistication 4. Innovation

g
- Read aloud the two examples and make sure students understand what the two expressions mean. Point out that hyphenated expressions like these are called compound adjectives and that they are common in English. Also point out that advertisers often invent new, colorful expressions for describing their products.
- Have students work alone or in pairs matching words from Box A and Box B to make compound adjectives. Check answers. Draw to students' attention the alliterative nature of phrases like *cost-cutting, long-lasting,* and *space-saving*. Point out that alliterative phrases are often used in advertising because they are more memorable.

> **Answers**
> mouth-watering, customer-friendly, trouble-free, energy-saving, well-known, family-size, cost-cutting, space-saving, user-friendly, multi-purpose, long-lasting

h
- Ask students to study the information in the chart. Then have students add two more examples (taken from the world of advertising) in each column.
- Check answers. Then, as necessary, review the rules for forming comparative adjectives.

i
- Read aloud the first pair of items and elicit sentences that compare the two things, for example, *An economy car is cheaper than a sports utility vehicle.*
- Then have students work alone or in pairs comparing the pairs of items. Encourage them to write three sentences for each pair and to try to use a mixture of the comparative forms from the chart in the previous activity. Ask individual students to read their answers aloud. Discuss the most interesting sentences with the whole group.

j
- Read aloud the instructions and make sure that students understand the task. Have them write drafts of their work and work in pairs checking and correcting them before they write out a final version.
- Invite individual students to read their work aloud.

Lesson 2

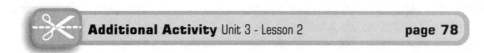

Additional Activity Unit 3 - Lesson 2   page 78

Answers
1. 1. When was Sunny Delight first launched? 2. How was Sunny Delight marketed? 3. And was it really a healthy drink? 4. What happened to the product.
2. Answers will vary.

Writing Resource 3A   page 102

This task asks students to research and present written report on the history, development, and present status of a world-famous brand and /or logo.

Lesson 3 Finding out what appeals . . .   SB Pages 34–35

In this lesson, students learn about marketing strategies and about market research. After an initial discussion activity, students study common collocations from the world of marketing. Some of this vocabulary appears in the reading comprehension task that follows. Students then discuss the subject of market research. They listen to a talk about data collection techniques and then put these ideas into practice in a guided simulation activity.

a
- With books closed, ask students to give the names of stores, shopping centers, supermarkets, etc. that they like to visit, not for the merchandise on sale, but for the qualities and characteristics of the places themselves. Invite students to describe their favorite places to shop and to explain what it is that they like about these places.
- Ask students to open their books and to read the discussion questions. Organize students into pairs and have them discuss the questions. Open up the topics for whole-class discussion.

b
- Review briefly the concept of collocations — words that are often used together in relatively fixed combinations. Read aloud one of the words from Box A, e.g. *marketing*, and elicit a word from Box B with which this word combines to form a familiar phrase, e.g. *marketing strategy*.
- Then have students work alone or in pairs forming more collocations from the words in Box A and Box B. Check answers.

> **Answers**
> marketing sector, marketing strategy, marketing techniques, electronically compatible, latest offers, latest designs, latest techniques, sales process, sales strategy, sales techniques, sales sector, business sector, business environment, special offers, special designs, special techniques, high standard, customer-friendly environment

c
- To begin, discuss the idea that every company has to decide how best to market and advertise its products. Then ask students to look at the photographs and to say what products are shown.
- Ask students to skim the text quickly for the main idea. Then have them read again carefully and match each of the descriptions of the companies with the marketing strategies listed in the box. Check answers.

> **Answers**
> 1. c   2. a   3. d   4. b

d
- Ask students to read the questions. Then organize students into pairs or small groups and have them discuss the questions. Discuss students' ideas as a whole class.
- Invite pairs of students to perform a quick representation of a typical person-in-the-street market research survey.

CD T-22

e
- With books closed, tell students that they are going to listen to a talk on the subject of data collection for market research. Have students listen to the audio once through for the general idea.
- Then ask students to open their books and to look at the information in the chart. Have students listen to the talk again and complete the chart by marking each technique as Primary or Secondary. Check answers.

> **Answers**
> Primary: Using questionnaires to find out people's likes and dislikes, Observing people as they shop in a store, Conducting face-to-face interviews with consumers, Conducting consumer panels on TV and radio
> Secondary: Analyzing companies' sales reports, Checking newspapers and government reports, Analyzing industry trade figures, Searching the Internet for data

Lesson 3

f
- To begin, start a discussion about coffee — the types of coffee that are commonly sold in stores and also the types of coffee that are available in cafes and coffee shops. Elicit information about the availability of organic coffee in the students' country. Ask if it is grown there or if it is imported from other countries.
- Ask students to read the instructions. Make sure they understand the three data collection methods mentioned. Have students work alone listing the advantages and disadvantages of each method, taking into account the factors in the box plus their own ideas. Make sure that students understand the difference between preparation time, the time it actually takes to collect the data, and analysis time.

g
- Organize students into small groups and have them compare and discuss their ideas. Ask them to try to arrive at a consensus regarding the best data collection method for this product.
- Invite different groups to share their ideas and ask them to give reasons for their choices.

h
- By a quick show of hands, find out how many people chose personal interviews as the best data collection technique. Review the advantages and disadvantages of this method.
- Then ask students to work alone writing questions that they would include in a market research questionnaire about consumer's opinions, attitudes, etc, about organic coffee or about some other product. Ask students to write at least five questions.

i
- Organize students into pairs and have them share, compare, and discuss their questions. Encourage students to help each other to improve the wording of their questions, for example, to make them more specific, less ambiguous, etc.
- As a whole class, discuss the importance of wording market research questions carefully so as to obtain as much useful information as possible.
- As extension, invite groups of students to compile their questions in complete questionnaires and to carry out their own surveys about products of their choosing. Ask students to analyze their results and to present their findings for the rest of the group.

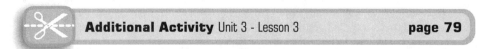
Additional Activity Unit 3 - Lesson 3   page 79

Answers
1. 1. customer 2. achieve 3. analysis 4. attitudes 5. purchasing 6. population 7. brand 8. relationship
2. Answers will vary.

Reading Resource 3A   page 91

Students read an article about the history and development of marketing. They scan the text for specific information and then answer comprehension questions. Language work focuses on word formation.

Answers
A Early Concepts in Marketing
B 1. 1920s 2. Bohm-Bawerk 3. Paul W. Ivey 4. 1930s 5. Paul D. Converse
C 1. performance 2. direct 3. producers 4. satisfy

Writing Resource 3B   page 101

In this task, students prepare a series of questions for a questionnaire designed to elicit customers' reactions to a chosen product or service.

Lesson 4 You too can do it—having a plan   SB Pages 36–37

In the first half of this lesson, students find out more about marketing, in particular about four different marketing strategies. Vocabulary and discussion work lead into a reading task and listening tasks that, in turn, lead to more vocabulary work. The grammatical focus of the lesson, in the second half, is the present perfect especially as contrasted or combined with the simple past. In the latter part of the lesson, students look at e-mail communication and consider the question of appropriate register.

a
- With books closed, write the following words on the board: *ambush, guerrilla, virus, blitz*. Ask students to say what they think these words mean but do not give them any correct answers at this stage.
- Ask students to open their books and to read the expressions in the box. Have students work in pairs, using dictionaries if necessary, discussing the meaning of these terms in the context of marketing. Discuss answers as a whole group.

b
- Ask students to skim through the text quickly for the general idea.
- Then have them read again more carefully and complete each section with the correct term from the previous exercise. Check answers.
- Draw to students' attention the fact that three of these terms *(guerilla, blitz, ambush)* are direct borrowings from the vocabulary of warfare and that all four terms carry strong connotations of aggressive conduct. Invite students to comment on this.

> **Answers**
> 1. guerilla marketing 2. blitz marketing 3. viral marketing 4. ambush marketing

CD T-23 **c**
- Ask students to listen to the audio once right through for the general idea.
- Then play the track again pausing after each speaker to give students time to identify which marketing strategy is being exemplified in each case. Check answers. Then elicit examples of similar real-life cases that students have heard about.

> **Answers**
> Company #1: guerilla marketing, Company #2: blitz marketing, Company # 3: ambush marketing, Company # 4: viral marketing

CD T-24 **d**
- Read aloud the words and phrases. Then ask students to listen to the audio again and to find words that mean the same (or nearly the same) as these expressions.
- Check answers and then discuss with students the fact that perfectly interchangeable synonyms are, in fact, quite rare and there is normally some slight and subtle but possibly significant change in the meaning of a sentence when one word is substituted with another. Illustrate this point referring to the words featured in the exercise.

> **Answers**
> makes something easier: facilitates / introduction of new product: launch / persuading: convince / expectation: anticipation / completely covered: plastered / unwilling: involuntary / approval: endorsement

e
- Read aloud the first item and ask students to say which sounds better: *He designed some new graphics software...* or *He has designed some new graphics software....*If students are not sure, ask them to look at the time reference at the end of the sentence. Point out or elicit that the expression, *over the past few*

Lesson 4

months connects the past to the present and implies that, in all probability, he is still designing graphics software and will continue to do so. Thus, the most appropriate verb tense in this instance is the present perfect.

- Have students work alone completing the rest of the exercise. Point out to students that if they think that there are two possible answers, they should write both. Check answers.

> **Answers**
> 1. has designed 2. started, has grown 3. began, has increased 4. has received / received 5. has expanded

f
- Ask students to compare and discuss their answers to the previous exercise and to mark the sentence(s) where either the simple past or the present perfect could be used.
- Check and discuss answers. Explain in item 4, one could use either tense since no specific time reference is mentioned. Ask students to say which tense would be correct if the sentence were: *I hope everybody _____ a copy of the agenda yesterday.* (simple past)

g
- Ask students to glance briefly at the e-mail. Establish that it is an internal communication and that it is about a meeting that is to take place in the future.
- Ask students to read through the questions and then to check the e-mail more carefully and answer the questions. Check answers.

> **Answers**
> 1. She forgot to mention the date of the meeting. 2. The tone of the e-mail is not appropriate. It is too informal.

h
- Discuss the inappropriateness of Lisa's e-mail and discuss in general the importance of adopting the appropriate register for any given situation.
- Ask students to rewrite the e-mail in their notebooks using the words and expressions in the box if they choose. Make clear to students that they can add or remove material as they see fit but that the message must contain all the necessary detail and be expressed in the correct register.
- Invite students to read their corrected e-mails aloud the rest of the group.

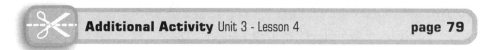

Additional Activity Unit 3 - Lesson 4   page 79

Answers
1. 1. install 2. growth 3. development 4. exclusion 5. endorsement 6. convincing 7. anticipation 8. expect 9. approve 10. originality
2. Answers will vary.

Reading Resource 3B   page 92

This task requires students to read a text about the Benetton company for general ideas in order to match headings with paragraphs. Students then complete a true / false exercise.

Answers
A Answers will vary.
B 1. The Company 2. The Creative Director 3. Controversy 4. Consequences
C 1. False 2. True 3. False 4. False 5. True

Lesson 5 Getting together and . . .   SB Pages 38–39

This lesson combines more information about marketing with activities that give students useful practice in skills that they will need in the workplace, in particular, with regard to meetings. The lesson begins with discussion and listening activities about meetings. Students then work on reading comprehension and vocabulary activities before tackling another listening. Through discussion and role play activities, students practice making requests using appropriate language and register.

a
- With books closed, start a discussion about meetings. In particular, find out how many students ever attend meetings and, if so, how often these meetings take place, how long they usually last, how they are carried out, etc.
- Ask students to open their books. Organize them into pairs and have them make a list of typical reasons why people hold meetings. Then open up the discussion for the whole group. As appropriate, share some information with students regarding how often teachers at their school attend meetings, when and where these meetings take place, how long they normally last, etc.

b
- With books closed, discuss the fact that not everyone enjoys attending meetings. Elicit ideas about why a person might not feel very enthusiastic about attending a meeting. Tell students that they are going to hear a conversation in which two people talk about an upcoming meeting and share their views about meetings in general. Ask students to listen to the conversation once through for the main idea.
- Have students open their books. Ask them to look at the notes and then to listen to the audio again and to complete the notes with the relevant details. Check answers and then elicit responses to what students heard in the conversation.

> **Answers**
> 1. talk things over face to face 2. clear up some ambiguous issues 3. keep us well-briefed on new proposals and developments 4. included in decision-making 5. opportunities to give our feedback 6. be involved in planning input our ideas

c
- Organize students into pairs and have them discuss the meaning of the expressions in the box, which all feature in the conversation they heard previously.
- Check and discuss answers. Elicit sentences that illustrate the meaning of each expression.

d
- Elicit the meaning of the term *life cycle* in nature. Then review the concept of life cycles in the context of business activity.
- Set a time limit and have students skim through the text quickly and match each paragraph with the correct heading. Check answers.

> **Answers**
> 1. Development 2. Growth 3. Maturity 4. Decline

e
- Ask students to read the text again, more carefully this time, and have them work alone writing definitions of the words and phrases in the box.
- Ask students to compare and discuss their answers in pairs. Check answers as a whole class.

Lesson 5

> **Answers**
> loses appeal: is no longer attractive to customers
> levels off: remains the same and does not increase
> ceases: stops
> downward spiral: sales drop quickly
> take off stage: time when sales of a product increase rapidly

- With books closed, elicit ideas about the logistics of meetings in a business environment. Ask students to imagine that they wish to call a meeting. Ask, *How do you tell people about the meeting? How much notice should you give people? What information do you give them about the meeting? How do you make sure that they attend?*
- Ask students to open their books and to read the questions. Then have students listen to the conversation and answer the questions. Check answers.

> **Answers**
> 1. An upcoming meeting 2. a secretary and a boss

- Ask students to listen to the conversation again carefully and to number the points on the agenda in the correct order according to what they hear in the conversation.
- Check answers and deal with any questions that students may have regarding standard procedure for formal meetings. If necessary, explain the terms *minutes* and *any other business*, often abbreviated to AOB.

> **Answers**
> 1. Read the minutes of the last meeting 2. Any matters arising out of minutes 3. Welcome new staff members 4. Apologies for absences 5. Organizing marketing research — preparation of questionnaires 6. Budget arrangements for product 7. Sales forecasts and targets 8. Planned timeframe for research and analysis 9. Any other business

h
- Read aloud the questions. Then organize students into pairs and have them discuss the questions.
- Then open up the discussion for the whole group. Elicit and write up on the board a selection of expressions that are commonly used when someone makes a request. Focus in particular on the use of the modal verbs *can*, *could*, and *would* and on the use of the imperative.

i
- Ask students to read through the information on the role cards. Make sure that students understand the situations. Organize students into pairs and have them select a situation and work on a short role play. Encourage students to use appropriate language—taking into account both grammatical structure and the appropriate tone—when making requests.
- Invite pairs of students to present their role plays to the rest of the group. Invite observation and comment about the language that students used and how effectively they handled their chosen situations.

Additional Activity Unit 3 - Lesson 5   page 80

Answers
1. formal expressions: meeting, would like to apologize, unable to attend, previous commitment, contact you, unfortunately, inform you
   informal expressions: just to let you know, real sorry, something else on, give you a buzz, see you later, can't make it, get together
2. Answers will vary.

Unit 3

Lesson 6 If you can make it, . . .   SB Pages 40–41

The topic of this lesson is the global problem of pirated merchandise, that is, the illegal copying and selling of well-known brands, and the infringement of copyright that this represents. Students begin with discussion and vocabulary activities. They then tackle a series of listening tasks. The language focus of the lesson is multiword verbs and their equivalents. At the end of the lesson, students write about the problem of pirated goods and they practice using connecting phrases in sentences that show cause and effect.

a
- With books closed, discuss the basic, original meaning of the word *pirate*. Elicit ideas about pirates of former times, be they historical figures or characters from fiction. Establish the key idea that piracy in former times was essentially a type of theft of someone else's goods or property.
- Ask students to open their books and have them read the discussion questions. Organize students into pairs and have them discuss the questions. Then open up the discussion for the whole group.

b
- Ask students to look at the phrases in the box and to write a check mark next to the ones that they definitely know the meaning of. If students think that they know the meaning but are not 100% sure, they should mark their doubt about these words accordingly.
- Explain to students that the meanings of some of the words in this box will become clear as they proceed through the lesson. Point out to students that it is not unusual for even native speakers of English to come across terms that they do not understand or that they may have some doubt about, especially in texts containing specialized, technical vocabulary. Point out that in many instances, the meaning of an unfamiliar term becomes clear as one continues to read or listen.

CD T-28

c
- Ask students to listen to the audio once through for the general idea and without writing anything down.
- Then have them look briefly at the notes before listening again and completing the notes with the correct information. Check answers.

> **Answers**
> 1. property rights   2. 5-7%   3. $512 billion   4. 10%

CD T-29

d
- First discuss the fact that pirating is a worldwide problem. Then ask students to listen to the next part of the talk and to match each country with the pirated goods that are mentioned.
- Check answers and invite observation and comment.

> **Answers**
> 1. b 2. e 3. a 4. b 5. c

CD T-30

e
- Ask students to read through the questions so that they know what to listen for. Ask students to listen to the last part of the talk and then to work in pairs answering the questions.
- Check and discuss the answers. Then review the whole sequence of listening material — playing the audio again if necessary—and elicit observation and comment. Encourage students to share their ideas.

Lesson 6   41

> **Answers**
> 1. China 2. because of international pressure 3. putting pressure on governments

f
- Review the words and phrases that students saw in Exercise b. Ask for instances of words or phrases that individual students were not sure about but which they now understand clearly having heard the expressions being used in context.
- Then deal with any outstanding questions that students may still have regarding vocabulary.

g
- Review the fact that, invariably, phrasal verbs—common in conversational English—can be substituted with more formal, single-word equivalents. Illustrate this by reading aloud the first item in the exercise.
- Then have students work alone or in pairs completing the rest of the exercise. Make sure that students understand that it may be necessary to modify the form of certain verbs. Check answers.

> **Answers**
> 1. increased 2. accounts for 3. results in 4. heard 5. discovered 6. produced 7. control 8. find

h
- Ask students to read through both sets of sentence parts. Elicit or point out that at the beginning of many of the fragments there is a phrase that indicates that something is being explained, e.g. expressions like *due to the fact that*, *and so*, and *consequently*, etc. Read aloud the whole sentence given as an example. Make sure that students understand the way the phrase *and so* indicates an explanation of a cause and an effect.
- Ask students to work alone or in pairs reading the sentences carefully and matching the corresponding parts. Check answers and review the connecting expressions used in this exercise.

> **Answers**
> 1. d 2. g 3. f 4. b 5. e 6. c 7. a

i
- Have students do some research about the problem of pirated goods and to write a short report. Ask them to include connecting phrases like the ones used in this lesson to express cause-and-effect relationships.
- Invite individual students to read their sentences aloud.

Additional Activity Unit 3 - Lesson 6   page 80

Answers
1. 1. c 2. f 3. d 4. a 5. e 6. b
2. Answers will vary.

Team Project 3

Prepare a report about a franchise opportunity SB Page 42

- Organize students into groups of four or five. Read aloud the instructions and make sure that students understand what they are to do. If necessary, spend a little time explaining what franchises are and how they generally work.
- Ask students what sort of businesses in their country are run under a franchise system. Invite observation and comment.
- Have students prepare their reports. Encourage them to make their reports as full and informative as possible and to include any relevant visual aids such as photographs, diagrams, charts, tables, graphs, etc. when they present their findings.

Review 3

SB page 74

Answer Key

A
1. can be marketed 2. will be designed 3. was invented 4. was carried out

B (Suggested answers.)
1. You should come to the movies with us tonight. 2. I really think we ought to postpone the marketing meeting. 3. You must work overtime if you want to finish that project. 4. I don't think you should miss this opportunity. 5. I need you to help me to fix my computer. It should be really easy for you.

C
1. exceeded/have not reached 2. works/has worked 3. has just arrived/wants/sounds
4. went/is/hasn't had/hasn't yet eaten

D
1. more successful than 2. more popular than 3. as well-known as 4. as hard as
5. more powerful than

Unit 4

Financial Matters

Objectives

Language skills: brainstorming and evaluating ideas, listening for specific information, discussing ideas, listening and taking notes, writing about future events, identifying text types, reading for specific information, writing definitions of words, writing a business letter, listening for numerical information, understanding vocabulary from context, formulating questions, role-playing situations, writing reports, summarizing information, using formal and informal registers, using business jargon and business slang

Functions: speculating about the future, making predictions, expressing opinions, talking about advantages and disadvantages

Grammar: *will* for future possibilities, modals for obligation, advice, recommendation, etc., miscellaneous question forms

Lesson 1 Keeping a record of personal expenses   SB Pages 44–45

This lesson is about students' expenses for a typical year away at college. First, students brainstorm and discuss ideas. Then there is a series of activities in which students listen to and discuss information about a student's calculations of her expenses. Students use appropriate language for making speculations and predictions. These activities are followed by a role play about expected expenditure and the lesson finishes with a writing task in which students use various modal structures to express possibility, obligation, etc.

a
- With books closed, start a discussion on the subject of students who live at home while they attend college compared with those who live away from home. Ask students which situation is more common in their country. Invite comment and discussion about the advantages and disadvantages of each situation. Ask students whether they prefer / would prefer to live at home or live away from home while at college.
- Ask students to open their books and to look at the first activity. Have students brainstorm ideas in pairs or small groups about the expenses that college students have when they live away from home. Then open up the discussion for the whole group and elicit a number of suggestions.

b (CD T-31)
- Tell students that they are going to hear two students discussing and comparing the expenses that they expect to have while away at college. Ask them to look at the chart. Elicit or explain the meaning of the term *utilities* (household services like electricity, water, gas).
- Have students listen to the whole conversation once through for the general idea. Then play the audio again and have students complete the chart with the missing information (headings and amounts). Check answers.

> **Answers**
> **Michelle:** Tuition: 500; Rent: 400; Utilities: 0; Food: 100; Textbooks: 300; Clothes: 0; Transport: 50; Recreation: 30
> **Roger:** Tuition: 500; Rent: 400; Utilities: 50; Food: 70; Textbooks: 150; Clothes: 0; Transport: 50; Recreation: 30

c
- Explain to students that they are going to hear another student talking about the income that she expects to have for the coming year, when she plans to do an MBA in **d**. Ask them to look at the items in the chart. Elicit speculative ideas about how much money students think Anne will have saved from her summer job. Encourage students to make an "educated guess", bearing in mind Anne's probable age and the sort of summer jobs that would be available.
- Arrange students in pairs and have them speculate about the other items in Anne's list and complete the first column in the chart. Encourage them to use the sentence openers provided in the box.

- Play the audio and have students complete the second column of the chart with the correct figures.
- Organize students into new pairs and have them compare and discuss the estimates they made earlier with the real figures. Invite comment and discussion.

> **Answers**
> **Saved earnings from summer job:** $2,500; **Part-time work during coming year:** $2,500; **Savings:** $1,000; **Grants:** $1,000; **Other income:** $2,000; **Total income for academic year:** $9,000

- With books closed, discuss briefly the basic idea of income and expenditure. Elicit examples of situations where there is income and expenditure and discuss the importance of balancing the two, i.e. not letting expenditure exceed income.
- Ask students to open their books and have them look briefly at Anne's list of monthly expenses. Ask students to explain why they think her monthly total is multiplied by 10 and not by 12.
- Play the audio one or two times and have students complete the notes with the correct amounts. Check answers.

> **Answers**
> **Rent:** $400; **Books / School supplies:** $300; **Food / Household supplies:** $350; **New clothes:** 0; **Entertainment:** $50; **Telephone:** $40; **Transportation:** $20; **Total monthly expenses:** $1,160; **Total annual expenses:** $11,600

f
- Read aloud the first question and elicit answers. Then organize students into pairs and have them discuss the remaining questions.
- Discuss answers as a whole-class activity.

g
- Read aloud the sample questions. Draw to students' attention the combination of the future with *will* and expressions using *I think* . . . Point out that this is a common way of expressing ideas that cannot be quantified with 100% precision.
- Organize students in to groups of three or four and have them role-play conversations in which they ask for and provide information about their expected expenditure.
- Invite various groups to share their role plays with the rest of the class. As an alternative, have students role play conversations in pairs on this same topic but ask one of the students to take the role of a parent.

h
- Read aloud the expressions in the box. Elicit or point out that these expressions use modal constructions to express various concepts, e.g. obligation, possibility, recommendation, etc.
- Ask students to first write some notes and then to work these notes up into a paragraph about their expenditure for a year's study away from home. Encourage students to use expressions like the ones provided in the box. Also, encourage students to read each other's work and to suggest improvements before writing out a final version.

i
- Organize students into new pairs and have them share, compare, and discuss their ideas about their expected expenditure.
- Invite individual students to read their work aloud for the rest of the group.

 Additional Activity Unit 4 - Lesson 1   **page 81**

Answers
1. 1. "Extra" expenses 2. Used books 3. Consider a roommate 4. Work while at college

Lesson 2 Starting out

SB Pages 46–47

This lesson deals with the subject of bank accounts and credit cards, especially from the point of view of a first-time applicant such as a student. The lesson begins with a discussion activity followed by reading comprehension tasks. Students then focus on vocabulary and discuss questions of style and tone in the advertising material featured in the reading. The lesson finishes with a listening activity and a letter-writing

a
- With books closed, elicit the names of well-known banks in the students country. Ask students to share what they know about these banks. Also, elicit recent news items related to individual banks or to the banking system in their country.
- Ask students to open their books and to read the discussion questions. Then have students discuss the questions in pairs. Invite students to share their ideas, opinions, comments, etc. with the rest of the group.

b
- With books closed, elicit examples of the different ways that banks advertise their services. Ask for real examples from TV commercials, magazine and newspaper ads, etc.
- Ask students to just look at the brochure as a whole rather than simply read the text. In particular, draw to students' attention elements like the photographs used and the style and layout of the text. Read aloud the questions and have students discuss them in pairs.

c
- Read aloud the questions. Then ask students to read through the text carefully and, working alone, to make notes of the answers to the questions.
- Ask students to work in pairs comparing and discussing their answers. Then open up the discussion for the whole group. Invite students to share information about special student deals or offers that banks have advertised recently.

d
- Read aloud the first item and elicit a definition of the word as it is used in the text on the previous page.
- Then have students work alone or in pairs writing definitions for the remaining words, using a dictionary if necessary. Point out to students that the first definition that appears in a dictionary may not be the one that best fits the meaning of the word as it is used in the reading text. Check answers and then, as an extension activity, ask students to write sentences in their notebooks illustrating the meaning of each word in this exercise.

> **Answers**
> 1. shared by both parties 2. a person who runs his / her own business 3. something offered to a lender as security for a loan 4. to take out money from one's bank account 5. fees that account holders pay for bank services 6. the amount of money in a person's bank account at a given time

e
- Refer students back to the advertising material on the previous page. Ask students: *Does this text have a formal or an informal style?*
- Organize students into pairs or small groups and have them discuss the style and tone of the text and to identify those elements (vocabulary, expressions, contractions, etc.) that make the text sound informal.
- Then discuss why the bank decided to adopt this tone for their promotional material. Elicit examples of other advertising campaigns that students have seen that try to appeal to young consumers by adopting an informal tone or style.

Unit 4

CD T-34

- With books closed, discuss the subject of credit cards, in particular, in relation to students / young people in their country. Ask students if they have ever been approached by a bank asking them to apply for a credit card. Invite them to share their experiences and impressions.
- Ask students to open their books and to look at the notes. Have them listen to the audio once through for the general idea. Then play the audio again and have them complete the notes with the correct information. Check and discuss answers.

> **Answers**
> for booking airline tickets
> fill out a form, obtain manager's approval
> make partial payment, pay balance in full, pay fixed amount at fixed intervals
> partial payment each month on what is owed
> $40
> 18%

- Discuss with students the problems that can arise when young people are issued credit cards. As appropriate, elicit real-life cases that students have heard about involving young people or students who had problems with credit card debt.
- Ask students to look briefly at the letter. Make sure they understand what it is about. Then have students work alone drafting a reply to the letter. Remind them that the tone and register of their letters should be formal. Encourage students to read each other's work and to suggest improvements before writing out a final version.

Additional Activity Unit 4 - Lesson 2   page 81

Answers
1. 1. d 2. g 3. c 4. f 5. a 6. b 7. e
2. Answers will vary.

Reading Resource 4A   page 93

Students read an article about recent developments in banking systems and operations and complete a variety of reading comprehension tasks. They use contextual clues to understand vocabulary items.

Answers
A 1. They have increased the scope and scale of their activities. They have become very large institutions through mergers and takeovers. 2. Innovations in communication have made the U.S. economy much more integrated. 3. They are subject to the same market pressure to become national.
B 1. ascent 2. dividing 3. look 4. ration 5. leader 6. relaxed
C Answers will vary.
D Answers will vary.

Writing Resource 4A   page 102

This activity asks students to write a letter requesting a grant to cover the cost of an MBA. They explain why they want to study for an MBA, they outline the business area that interests them, and they describe their long-range plans

Lesson 3 Managing expenses   SB Pages 48–49

In this lesson, the focus shifts from the income and expenditure of an individual to the financial and accounting side of a business. Students begin with discussion and vocabulary activities focusing on specific terms used in finance. They then listen to some financial information and do some calculations. In the second half of the lesson, students read about a dot com company that went bust. Activities consist of reading comprehension, vocabulary work, and a discussion task.

a
- Write on the board the following sets of initials and ask students to say what they stand for: *CEO, CFO*. Elicit or explain that CEO means Chief Executive Officer while the letters CFO stand for Chief Financial Officer. Explain that the CFO of a company is the person who is primarily responsible for managing the financial risks of the business and who is also responsible for financial planning and record-keeping. Point out that another name for CFO is Finance Director.
- Read aloud the discussion questions. Then arrange students in pairs or small groups and have them discuss the questions. Then open up the topic for a whole-class discussion.

b
- Read aloud the first definition and elicit the word or phrase from the box that best matches it (debtor). Then have students work on pairs completing the rest of the exercise. Check and discuss answers.
- Discuss with students the question of business terminology, which can be complicated. Ask students to suggest resources or places where they can find definitions and explanations of business terms, e.g. dictionaries of business English, specialized web sites, etc.

> **Answers**
> 1. debtor 2. capital 3. creditor 4. inflation 5. fixed assets 6. balance sheet 7. current assets 8. liabilities

CD T-35

c
- Read aloud the instructions. Review the meaning of the term balance sheet, i.e. a statement of a company's financial condition at a given date. Ask students to listen to the audio once through without taking any notes.
- Then play the audio again and have students listen carefully and complete the balance sheet with the correct figures. Check answers and, if necessary review the meaning of the terms that appear on the balance sheet (fixed assets, current assets, current liabilities, etc.).

> **Answers**
> **Buildings:** $400,000; **Equipment:** $50,000; **Motor Vehicles:** $60,000; **Total:** $510,000; **Stock:** $7,000; **Cash:** $2,000; **Trade debtor:** $5,000; **Total:** $14,000; **Bank overdraft:** $2,500; **Trade creditors:** $800; **Total:** $3,300

d
- Have students take the relevant information from the completed balance sheet and use it to calculate the company's working capital and its total net assets.
- Check and discuss answers.

> **Answers**
> **Working capital:** $10,700
> **Total net assets:** $520,700

Lesson 3

e
- With books closed, elicit the names of some successful dot com companies, that is, companies that operate exclusively or chiefly on the Internet and that usually have names ending with the suffix .com, which identifies them as commercial organizations.
- Ask students to open their books and to look at the text. Elicit that it is a magazine article about a company called Itsbuzzin.com. Make sure that students understand that this name comes from an informal phrase, *It's buzzin'*, which people sometimes use to describe a heightened level of activity, interest, excitement, etc. Have students skim through the article briefly to get a grasp of the main idea. Finally, have them read the True/False statements. Then ask students to read the article again, more carefully, and to mark the statements as True or False. Check answers.

> **Answers**
> 1. False 2. True 3. True 4. False 5. False 6. True

f
- Discuss the fact that this article, like many that students will come across in the world of business, contains some difficult vocabulary. Remind students about the idea of working out the meaning of an unfamiliar word or phrase by using clues that are in the surrounding context.
- Arrange students into pairs and have them discuss the meaning of the words and phrases in the box. Check answers and then ask students to write definitions and sentences illustrating the meaning of each item.

g
- Organize students into pairs or small groups and have them discuss the questions about the rise and fall of Itsbuzzin.com.
- Then open up the discussion for the whole group, focusing on the topics that students find most interesting, most controversial, etc.
- As extension, invite students to research and present written reports about either a real dotcom that has been successful or about one that started in a promising fashion but then fell by the wayside. Invite individual students to share their reports with the rest of the group.

Additional Activity Unit 4 - Lesson 3   **page 82**

Answers
1. Answers will vary.
2. Answers will vary.

Lesson 4 Economic issues   SB Pages 50–51

Building on the previous lesson, students now consider larger issues that affect the economy of a nation as a whole—issues like inflation, prices, imports and exports, and the type of economy system that operates in a country. The lesson begins with discussion and vocabulary activities. Students then listen for some information about price increases and they calculate rates of inflation. The grammatical focus of the lesson is on question forms, which students practice by way of an interview. The lesson ends with pairwork and discussion activities and a writing task.

a
- With books closed, write on the board a selection of present-day prices of items that students habitually buy. Include things like CDs, soft drinks, candies, and items of clothing such as jeans, sneakers, etc. Also include other items such as bus fares and movie theater tickets. Then ask students how much these items cost five years ago. Elicit observation and comment on these changes.
- Ask students to open their books and to read the discussion questions. Then arrange students in pairs and have them discuss the questions. Finally, open up the topic for a whole-class discussion.

b
- Read aloud the first item and elicit the correct answer (c). Then have students work alone or in pairs matching the two halves of the sentences.
- Check and discuss answers.

> **Answers**
> 1. c 2. b 3. d 4. e 5. a

CD T-36

c
- Ask students to give examples of any items that have increased in price recently.
- Ask students to look at the chart. Tell them that they are going to hear some information about changes in prices between February and March. Play the audio and have students complete the chart with the correct information. Check answers.

> **Answers**
> **milk:** Feb $1.50, March $1.60; **yogurt:** Feb $2.50, March $2.50; **loaf of bread:** Feb $3.00, March $3.05; **sugar:** Feb $2.00, March $2.10; **apples:** Feb $4.00, March $4.20; **teabags:** Feb $2.20, March $2.30; **coffee:** Feb $4.00, March $3.50

d
- Review the answers to the previous activity. Ask: *Which items went up in price? Which prices stayed the same? Which prices went down?*
- Ask students to calculate the rate of inflation represented by the change in price of each individual item. Check answers.
- Then have students work in pairs discussing and predicting changes, if any, to the prices of the items in the chart. Discuss students' answers with the whole group.

> **Answers**
> milk: 6.6%; yogurt: 0%; loaf of bread: 1.7%; sugar: 5%; apples: 5%; teabags: 4.5%; coffee: 12.5%

Lesson 4

e
- With books closed, elicit the names of countries that students consider to be typical examples of a capitalist economy. Then ask: *Do all countries have this type of economic system? Which ones do not? What sort of system do they have?*
- Ask students to open their books and to skim briefly through the whole interview for the general idea. Then ask them to read the first question and answer. Have students work alone or in pairs writing appropriate questions for the remaining answers. Check answers and then ask students to practice the interview in pairs.

> **Answers**
> 1. Who makes decisions in a free enterprise system? 2. What things can people decide on when they set up a business? 3. What sort of decisions are made by the government in a centrally planned economy? 4. Can you give an example of a centrally planned economy? 5. What is a mixed economy? 6. Who makes the decisions in a mixed economy?

f
- Read aloud the discussion questions. Then arrange students in pairs or small groups and have them discuss the questions.
- Then open up the topic for a whole class discussion.

g
- Ask students to look at the chart. Make sure they understand the meaning of the term *commodity*. Ask students to say what they notice about the amounts of the commodities that are imported compared with the amounts that are exported.
- Organize students into pairs and have them analyze and discuss the information in the chart. Open up the discussion for the whole group and ask students to share their reactions to the data.
- Elicit ideas about how the situation in the UK compares with that of the students' own country. For example, ask: *Does this country import sugar? Does it export sugar? Which is greater, the amount that it imports or that it exports?*

h
- First, ask students to suggest resources or places where they can find information about imports and exports from their country.
- Ask students to prepare their written reports about the imported and exported commodities.
- As an alternative, if resources permit, ask students to prepare a multimedia presentation on this topic including spoken text, photographs, maps, charts, graphs, etc.

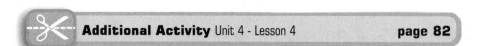

Answers
1. 1. price 2. income 3. economic 4. inverse 5. falls 6. direct 7. increases 8. demand 9. percentage 10. economists 11. elastic 12. inelastic
2. Answers will vary.

Students write a report describing and summarizing the key features of the economic system currently operating in their own country. They include information about the balance between free-market activity and state-run businesses, and they deal with such matters as rates of inflation, imports and exports, interest rates, etc.

Lesson 5 Investments

SB Pages 52–53

In this lesson, students learn about the world of investments. They begin the lesson with discussion and vocabulary activities and then they listen to an expert talking about different types of investments and the advantages and disadvantages of each type. Students then analyze and discuss information presented in a graph. Then students practice describing changes in a company's performance in terms of production, investment, profits, etc. To end the lesson, students work on vocabulary related to investments.

a
- With books closed, ask students to name cities around the world that are important financial centers, for example, New York City, London, Hong Kong, etc.
- Ask students to open their books and to look at the photograph. Have students discuss the questions in pairs or in small groups. Then open up the discussion for the whole group.

b
- Read aloud the first sentence and elicit the correct answer (stock). Then have students work alone or in pairs completing the remaining sentences with the correct words or phrases from the box.
- Check and discuss answers and then deal with any queries that students may have regarding vocabulary.

> **Answers**
> 1. stock 2. diversified portfolio 3. liquidity 4. volatility 5. fraud 6. hedge

c (CD T-37)
- Tell students that they are going to hear an expert giving information about different types of investment options. First have students look at the items listed in the first column of the chart. Elicit general information about these investment options.
- Have students listen to the talk once through for the general idea. Then ask students to listen again and to complete the chart with the correct information. Check answers. Finally, invite students to express their own opinions and preferences about the investment options. Ask: *How would you choose to invest your money? Why?*

> **Answers**
> **stocks and shares:** make a lot of money quickly (advantage); **bonds:** do not make a lot of money (disadvantage); **fixed-interest investments:** low levels of risk (advantage); **property:** cost of maintenance (disadvantage); **index futures:** chance of making large profits (advantage)

d
- Ask students to look at the graph and have them say what information it shows. Ask students to describe the graph as if they were explaining it to a layperson who has no specialized training in business.
- Have students work alone writing short summaries of the information shown in the graph. Then ask them to compare and discuss their summaries with those of their classmates.

e
- Organize students into new pairs and have them discuss which of the three options shown in the graph represented, in their opinion, is the best return on a $50,000 investment.
- Invite pairs of students to share their ideas and, in each case, have students justify their choices with reasons.

f
- Read aloud the example sentence. Then have students work alone or in pairs to complete the rest of the exercise.
- Check answers.

Lesson 5

> **Answers**
> 1. Profits from futures trading fell last year as competition hit commissions. 2. Astral Energy's acquisition of Star Oil boosted oil production by 32%. 3. Asset management made strong progress with profits of the firm up by 21% to 12 million. 4. Whizz turned in a good performance in the first quarter with Rowe's books selling strongly. 5. After lifting itself out of the red last year, BGH slipped back to register a loss of $8 million. 6. Shareholders have been put through the ringer due to the market's volatile behavior.

g
- Read aloud the first item from the box and ask students to say what it means. Ask them for the equivalent expression in their own language.
- Organize students into pairs and have them discuss the meaning of the other expressions in the box. Check answers and then deal with any outstanding queries that students may have regarding vocabulary.

h
- Discuss the importance of being able to communicate clearly not just with other experts in various fields of business but also with a layperson who has no specialized training in business.
- Ask students to write in their notebooks definitions of the terms highlighted in the previous exercise using simple language that a non-specialist could understand. Ask individual students to read their definitions aloud for the rest of the group. Invite comment.
- As extension, ask students to bring to their next class some newspaper cuttings or news items from the Internet about a company's current situation as expressed in the performance of its stock on the stock market, announcements about profits or losses in the current quarter, announcements about expansion plans or job cutbacks, etc.

Additional Activity Unit 4 - Lesson 5   page 83

Answers
1. 7, 2, 4, 6, 1, 8, 3, 9, 5
2. Answers will vary.

Reading Resource 4B   page 94

Students study some graphs showing information about personal loans, overdrafts, and savings and answer comprehension questions about this data. They then analyze some comments related to the information presented in the graphs.

Answers
A 1. True 2. True 3. False 4. False
B 1. As people get older, their debts and overdrafts go down and their savings increase.
   2. 65-year-olds 3. 49%

Lesson 6 Changes in the way we do things   SB Pages 54–55

The topic of this lesson is the global problem of pirated merchandise, that is, the illegal copying and selling of well-known brands, and the infringement of copyright that this represents. Students begin with discussion and vocabulary activities. They then tackle a listening task. The language focus of the lesson is multiword verbs and their equivalents. At the end of the lesson, students write about the problem of pirated goods and they practice using connecting phrases in sentences that show cause and effect.

a
- With books closed, refer students back to the previous lesson and elicit some technical terms that a financial expert would be expected to know but that many members of the general public who do not work in these fields would most likely not know. Ask students what this type of terminology is called, but do not give them the correct answer just yet.
- Ask students to open their books and to read the discussion questions. Have students discuss the questions in pairs. Then open up the discussion for the whole group. Elicit or explain that jargon is the special terminology of a particular activity or profession while slang is the informal, often invented vocabulary used principally in conversation often by members of a certain group. Mention the fact that slang expressions are sometimes considered vulgar or offensive by some people and that they are not normally used in any type of formal context, be it in speech or in writing.

b
- Read aloud the first item by way of example. Then have students work alone or in pairs matching the remaining expressions with the correct definitions.
- Check answers and then elicit ideas about the possible origins of some of these expressions. For example, ask: *Why is "sleeper" an appropriate term to describe a stock that is trading at an unusually low valuation? Why is the word "wallflower" used in this way?*

> **Answers**
> 1. d 2. j 3. f 4. e 5. i 6. h 7. b 8. a 9. g 10. c

  c CD T-38
- Start by eliciting any general information that students know concerning the traditional (i.e. pre-Internet) ways by which an individual could buy or sell stock. Ask them what they know about the mechanics of these transactions and also about the regulations governing such deals.
- Tell students that they are going to hear someone give information and advice about online investment trading. Have students look at the notes so that they know what to listen for. Then play the audio and have students complete the notes with the correct information. If necessary, play the audio again so that students can check their notes. Check answers.

> **Answers**
> **first essential step:** find out all you can before you begin
> **comparative studies:** do comparative studies of the kind of services available
> **instant placement:** wait for confirmation of the placement before doing anything else
> **investment:** set yourself a limit on the amount you invest

d
- Focus students' attention on the words and phrases in the box, all of which come from the listening.
- Have students work in pairs discussing the meaning of the expressions. Check answers and deal with any queries that students may have regarding vocabulary.

e
- Read aloud the discussion questions. Have students discuss the questions in pairs.
- Then open up the discussion for the whole group. Elicit a quick list of the sorts of business or financial transactions that nowadays can be carried out online and write some ideas on the board, for example, buying and selling merchandise, transferring funds, paying bills, checking bank statements, etc.

f
- Refer students back to Lesson 4 where, in exercise e, they completed an interview by supplying the missing questions. Have students skim briefly through the whole interview for the general idea. Then ask them to read the first question and answer.
- Have students work alone writing appropriate questions for the remaining answers.

g
- Organize students into pairs and have them compare and discuss the questions that they wrote. Ask them to focus not just on the content but also on the grammatical form of the questions.
- Check answers and then ask students to work in pairs role-playing conversations in which one person gives another person information and tips about online banking.

> **Answers**
> 1. I want to do my banking online. What do I need? 2. Can I pay my household bills online? 3. Can I arrange direct debit for regular bills? 4. How often can I check my account online? 5. How do I get paper records of my account? 6. Can I get information about loans online? 7. Is it possible to transfer funds electronically? 8. Is there ongoing customer service available? 9. How do I register for online banking?

h
- First, ask students to suggest resources or places where they can find information about online trading in stocks and online banking services.
- Ask students to prepare their written reports and to present them to the rest of the group.

Additional Activity Unit 4 - Lesson 6   page 83

Answers
1. 1. origins 2. evolved 3. tremendously 4. encouraged 5. expensive 6. participate 7. permitted 8. mobile 9. transaction 10. possibility
2. Answers will vary.

Team Project 4

Prepare a report about retail credit services SB Page 56

- Organize students into groups of four or five. Read aloud the instructions and make sure that students understand what they are to do. If necessary, spend a little time discussing various credit services - in particular retail credit from department stores - and how they generally work.
- Ask students for the names of department stores in their town or city that offer credit services to their customers. Invite observation and comment.
- Have students prepare their reports. Encourage them to make their reports as full and informative as possible and to include any relevant visual aids such as diagrams, charts, graphs, etc. when they present their findings.

Review 4

SB page 75

Answer Key

A

1. What time does the meeting begin? 2. How much does it cost to go to the staff party? 3. How many people work in the marketing department? 4. Why do I have to go the meeting? 5. Which report do you need?

B

Answers will vary.

C

1. bear in mind 2. trustworthy 3. maximize your profits 4. do your homework 5. placement

Unit 5

Global Concerns

Objectives

Language skills: discussing and evaluating ideas, reading for the gist, listening and taking notes, writing informal letters, understanding vocabulary from context, identifying synonyms, role-playing situations, reading for key ideas, writing reports, summarizing information, listening for specific information, reading for specific information, giving oral presentations, presenting information in graphs, word formation, listening to check information

Functions: expressing opinions, making requests, marking contrasts, reporting what someone says

Grammar: phrasal verbs, connecting phrases, prefixes for opposites, verb tenses, passive voice, reported speech

Lesson 1 Cultural issues   SB Pages 58–59

This lesson focuses on cultural issues, in particular on the experiences of a person living in and trying to adapt to differences in a foreign country. The first part of the lesson has students discussing material that they read about. They then work on some phrasal verbs featured in the reading material. Students then listen and take notes. More discussion questions and a writing task round off the lesson.

a
- With books closed, elicit the names of foreign companies, businesses, banks, etc. operating in the students' country. Have students speculate about the number of foreign workers currently employed with these companies. Also, elicit information about the number of foreign students currently taking courses at universities in the students' country.
- Ask students to open their books and have them read the discussion questions. Organize students into pairs or small groups and have them discuss the questions. Then open up the discussion for the whole group.

b
- Ask students to look at the two people in the photograph. Elicit or suggest the idea that one (it could be either one) of the two people is experiencing a new culture, i.e. the home culture of the other person. Ask students to imagine such a situation and to suggest some of the differences that the new person might have noticed between his / her new place of work and their own country.
- Ask students to look at the chart. Elicit or point out that the chart shows the steps in a process. Read aloud the terms in the box. Then ask students to say which expression from the box goes in the first space ("Honeymoon"). Then have students work alone or in pairs completing the rest of the chart. Check answers. If necessary, clarify the use of the term *honeymoon* to refer to the first phase.

> **Answers**
> "Honeymoon" phase, Transition phase, Understanding phase, Integration phase, Re-entry shock

c
- Read aloud one of the comments and ask students to say which of the phases in the chart it best corresponds to.
- Then have students work in pairs matching each of the remaining texts with the appropriate phase. Check and discuss answers.

> **Answers**
> Integration phase: "I'm beginning to feel more comfortable here . . . "
> "Honeymoon" phase: "It's so great to be here! I can't wait to . . . "
> Re-entry shock: "I feel so at home here now that . . . "
> Transition phase: "I'm so fed up with this place! The weather . . . "
> Understanding phase: "It's just like anywhere else - some things . . . "

d
- Have students look at the expressions on the left. Elicit or point out that these expressions are phrasal verbs. Remind students that phrasal verbs are very common, especially in spoken or more informal contexts.
- Read aloud the example answer and then ask students to work alone or in pairs matching each of the remaining phrasal verbs or fixed expressions with the correct meaning. Check answers.

> **Answers**
> 1. b 2. f 3. e 4. a 5. d 6. c

e
- With books closed, discuss briefly the idea that although many business transactions are essentially the same the world over, when people actually come into contact with other people from other cultures, that is where differences can become more apparent.
- Tell students that they are going to hear five people talking about their experiences working in another culture. Ask students to open their books and to look at the chart. Make sure that students understand that the first voice they will hear is that of a Chinese person living in the USA. Have them listen to the audio once through for the main ideas. Then ask them to listen again and to take notes of the key points that each speaker mentions. Check and discuss answers.

> **Answers**
> China/USA: Chinese more reserved, Americans outspoken, sense of humor
> UK/Saudi Arabia: dress conventions, eating with left hand; showing sole of shoe
> Japan/Brazil: level of formality, touching, relaxed, small talk
> USA/France: dress sense, attitude to time, language
> UAE/Australia: dress sense, punctuality, eye contact, direct speaking

f
- Read the questions aloud. Arrange students in pairs or small groups and have them discuss the questions.
- Then open up the discussion for the whole group.

g
- Make sure that students understand the term *pen pal*. Mention that the term *e-pal* is sometimes used to refer to pen pals that correspond via e-mail. Read aloud the instructions and make sure that students understand what they are to do.
- Have them write informal letters to an e-pal. Encourage students to read and comment on each other's letters.

Additional Activity Unit 5 - Lesson 1   **page 84**

Answers
1. 1. Do 2. Don't 3. Do 4. Do 5. Don't 6. Don't 7. Do 8. Don't 9. Do
2. Answers will vary.

Writing Resource 5A   **page 105**

For this task, students write a personal letter to a friend or family member in which they describe their (imaginary) experiences adapting to life and work in another country with a culture very different from that of their native country.

Lesson 2 Corporate culture   SB Pages 60–61

This lesson also deals with culture but the culture of a particular company rather than the culture of a country. First, students discuss the meaning of some key terms that they will use later in the lesson. This is followed by a listening task and then some reading material for discussion. Vocabulary work and a discussion task follow the reading. Students then listen to match the sentence openings and endings and the lesson finishes with a role play activity in which students practice language used for making requests.

a
- With books closed, open a discussion about corporate culture. Elicit ideas about what the term means and about how an organization's culture manifests itself in practical terms. Accept various tentative answers at this stage and explain that, as they work through the lesson, students will get a clearer idea about what corporate culture means.
- Have students open their books and ask them to read the discussion questions. Organize students into pairs or small groups and have them discuss the meaning of the two expressions. Then open up the discussion for the whole group.

CD T-40

b
- Start by directing students' attention to the illustration. Elicit observation and comment. Ask: *What is unusual about the way this man is dressed? What is he carrying? Why?* Then tell students that they are going to hear three people talking about the organizational culture of the different companies they work for.
- Ask students to listen to the audio once right through for the general idea. Then have them look at the chart on the page. Have students listen again and take notes of what each person says about the corporate culture of their company. Then ask students to match each employee with the most appropriate term from the box. Check and discuss answers.

> **Answers**
> Dave: open-plan, constant bustle and noise = Open and inclusive
> Marcia: assessing reaction of candidates = Innovative
> Omar: top controlled, no chance to make decisions = Authoritarian

c
- With books closed, write the following company names on the board. Winthrop Travel, California Coolers, Worldwide Bank. Have students speculate tentatively about the sorts of companies they are, how large or small they are, and what sort of organizational culture they have.
- Ask students to open their books and to read the information about the three companies. Organize students into pairs or small groups and have them discuss which types of organizational culture they think each company exemplifies. Discuss students' ideas.

d
- Read aloud the first item and then elicit any other words that students know that are related to the word *inherit*, for example *inheritance*.
- Then have students work alone or in pairs completing the rest of the exercise. Check answers.
- As extension, elicit other words related to the words that students found in the texts, for example, *insistence, interference, encouragement,* etc.

> **Answers**
> 1. inherit 2. insist 3. interfere 4. encourage 5. reflect 6. outsider 7. novel 8. challenging

Unit 5

e
- Organize students into pairs and have them discuss their reactions to the companies they read about in the texts.
- Invite students to share anything they know about companies large or small in the place where they live and the types of organizational culture that each company exemplifies.

f CD T-41
- Ask students to look at the exercise. Elicit that these are not complete sentences but the endings of sentences.
- Ask students to listen to the audio once through for the general idea. Then have them listen again and match each sentence opening with the correct ending. Students might need more time between each item. In which case, pause the track briefly after each sentence. Check answers.

Answers
1. b 2. c 3. e 4. g 5. f 6. a 7. d

g
- Review some ideas about the organizational culture within a company. Focus, in particular, on the way directors and managers interact with the staff working beneath them.
- Read aloud the situations. Then organize students into pairs and have them work on role plays in which a manager delegates a task to an employee. Encourage students to make use of the expressions provided in the box.
- Invite various pairs of students to present their role plays for the rest of the class.

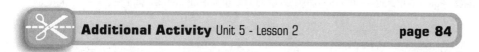

Additional Activity Unit 5 - Lesson 2   page 84

Answers
1. 1. b 2. d 3. a 4. c
2. Answers will vary.

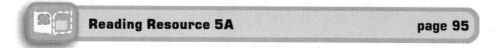

Reading Resource 5A   page 95

Students read short biographies of entrepreneurs who have created global enterprises. Students complete various comprehension tasks and vocabulary exercises.

Answers
A 1. Gates 2. Branson 3. Gates 4. Slim 5. Branson 6. Slim
B 1. False 2. False 3. True 4. False 5. True 6. True

Lesson 2

Lesson 3 Workplace changes   SB Pages 62–63

The focus of this lesson is changes in the workplace, in particular, two recent trends: employees working from home and companies outsourcing work to other companies. Discussion and listening activities open the lesson. Students then read a piece about outsourcing and then do some language work about connecting phrases. Another reading passage has students looking at paragraph divisions and they then summarize some information. A role play and a writing task round off the lesson.

a
- With books closed, do a quick show-of-hands survey to find out how many students have parents or other family members who work from home.
- Ask students to open their books and have them read the discussion questions. Organize students into pairs or small groups and have them discuss the questions. Then open up the discussion for the whole group.

b (CD T-42)
- Tell students that they are going to hear three people talking about the advantages and disadvantages of working at home or in an office. Have students listen to the whole audio once through for the general idea.
- Then play the audio again and have students take brief notes of the people's comments. Check answers.

> **Answers**
> **Marcus:** home – balance work time with workload, problem of communications sometimes, office – must spend 8 hours irrespective of workload
> **Paula:** home – advantage when one has children and it cuts out commuting, office – access to all resources
> **Jake:** home – saves money, office – able to monitor employees

c
- Read the discussion questions aloud. Organize students into pairs or small groups and have them discuss the questions.
- Then open up the discussion for the whole group. Encourage students to share with the rest of the group any recent information they have seen or heard about outsourcing.

d
- Set a time limit and have students skim through the article for the main ideas. Ask a few simple questions about the article to check students' understanding.
- Then ask students to read the article again more carefully and to find and underline five benefits of outsourcing that are mentioned in the text. Check and discuss answers.

> **Answers**
> Benefits: 1. cut costs   2. gain specialist knowledge   3. keep system up to date   4. no need to spend time and money   5. focus on core competencies

e
- Read aloud the first item in the exercise. Elicit other connecting expressions that express the idea of addition, for example, *as well as, in addition to, besides.*
- Then have students work alone or in pairs completing the rest of the exercise. Check answers. Then elicit other expressions that students know that can be used to express addition, cause and effect, and contrast.

> **Answers**
> 1. addition   2. contrast   3. contrast   4. cause and effect   5. addition   6. cause and effect

Unit 5

f
- First review the topic of paragraphs. Ask students to say why paragraphs are used and why they are important.
- Have students read through the text and mark where they think the second and third paragraphs should begin. Check and discuss answers. Discuss the fact that the sentence *However, some people have expressed . . .* is a good place to begin the third paragraph since it marks the change from advantages to potential disadvantages. However, this leaves the second paragraph very short and for this reason *There can also be infrastructure problems . . .* is also a good place to start the third paragraph since it marks a shift from the individual worker to the concerns of companies.

> **Answers**
> Paragraph 2: Why India? There is a large pool of . . .
> Paragraph 3: *either* However, some people have expressed . . . or There can also be infrastructure problems . . .

g
- Elicit some of the advantages and disadvantages of outsourcing in India.
- Then have students read through the text again and write notes in two columns, one for advantages and one for disadvantages.
- Encourage students to read each other's lists and to add their own ideas as well.

h
- Ask students to read the information on the role cards.
- Then organize students into pairs and have them role-play conversations based on this situation. Encourage students to take turns doing each of the two roles.
- Invite various pairs of students to share their role plays with the rest of the group.

i
- Read aloud the instructions. Ask students to do some research about a country like China, where outsourcing has become an important part of the economy. If relevant, have students include information about their own country.
- Encourage students to include graphs, charts, maps, and any other relevant visual support in their written reports.
- As an alternative, invite students to present their findings in a multimedia presentation for the rest of the group.

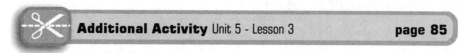

Additional Activity Unit 5 - Lesson 3   page 85

Answers
1. 8, 4, 2, 6, 1, 9, 7, 5, 3
2. Answers will vary.

Writing Resource 5B   page 106

In this activity, students take on the role of general manager of an insurance company and they write a letter to their CEO recommending that some of the company's tasks be outsourced to India. In their letters, they use appropriate language to express necessity and obligation.

Lesson 4 The other side of modern business   SB Pages 64–65

This lesson invites students to explore and discuss questions of ethics and legality in the world of business. Students begin with a discussion activity followed by listening and reading tasks. These are followed by exercises that focus on prefixes used for forming the opposites of adjectives. Then there is more language work about verb tenses and the lesson ends with another discussion activity and a research assignment.

a
- With books closed, share with students newspaper cuttings or printed reports from Internet news sources about any recent cases of scandal and fraud involving large corporations. Elicit observation and comment.
- Ask students to open their books and have them read the discussion questions. Organize students into pairs or small groups and have them discuss the questions. Then open up the discussion for the whole group.

b (CD T-43)
- Tell students that they are going to hear some information about Enron. Ask students to look briefly at the incomplete notes so that they know what to listen for.
- Play the audio and have students complete the notes with the correct information. Play the audio a second time if necessary. Check answers.

> **Answers**
> Houston, 2001, 21,000, $101 billion, 1996, 100, 2000, 4,000

c
- Set a time limit and have students skim through the text quickly. Then ask some questions to check their general understanding.
- Then read the comprehension questions aloud. Ask students to read through the article again and to answer the questions. Ask students to mark in the text the places where they found the information that they needed to be able to answer correctly. Check and discuss answers.

> **Answers**
> 1. pioneer marketing and the promotion of power commodities 2. accounting fraud 3. through mysterious and improper financial transactions

d
- With books closed, elicit pairs of opposite adjectives in the students' own language. Ask if there is any "system" for forming the opposite of an adjective.
- Ask students to open their books and to look at the words in the exercise. Read aloud the first item and ask students to find the opposite of this word in the text on the previous page (illegally).
- Then have students work alone or in pairs finding the opposites of the remaining adjectives. Check answers.

> **Answers**
> 1. illegally 2. unprofitable 3. irregular 4. nonexistent 5. improper

Unit 5

e
- Review the words in the previous exercise. Elicit or point out that in every case, the opposite of the adjective is formed by adding something at the beginning. Elicit or explain that this additional element at the start of a word is called a *prefix*.
- Ask students to look at the words in the box. Have them complete the chart by writing each adjective in the correct column according to the prefix that is added to it to form its opposite. Check answers.

Tell students that the prefix *in-* is also used for forming the opposites of certain adjectives *(invisible, indecisive,* etc.). Point out that the adjective *infamous* is not the opposite of *famous* but that it means *notorious* or "famous for the wrong reasons".

> **Answers**
> il-: illegible, illogical
> im-: impossible, imprudent
> ir-: irrational, irresponsible
> non-: noncommittal, nondiscriminatory
> un-: untruthful, unlawful

f
- Ask students to look at the verb structures listed on the left. Have them work in pairs looking through the text on the previous page to find at least one example of each of these verb structures.
- Check answers.

> **Answers**
> 1. revealed that 2. it was discovered 3. had created 4. has become

g
- Ask students to read through the four items. Focus their attention on the various expressions that refer to time. Elicit the correct form of the given verb in the first item (have affected) and discuss why the present perfect is used here.
- Then have students work alone or in pairs completing the remaining sentences. Check and discuss answers.

> **Answers**
> 1. have affected 2. declined 3. had inflated 4. have changed

h
- Read aloud the discussion topic. Organize students into small groups and have them discuss the topic.
- Then open up the discussion for the whole group. Encourage students to use appropriate modal verbs (can, should, must, etc.) to talk about the legal and moral responsibilities of corporations and governments.

i
- Remind students of some of the cases of corporate fraud mentioned earlier in the lesson. Have students work alone or in pairs researching and preparing oral reports about interesting cases that have been in the news recently.
- Alternatively, invite students to take on the role of investigative journalists and to present their findings in the form of a television documentary report.

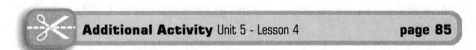

Additional Activity Unit 5 - Lesson 4   **page 85**

Answers
1. e 2. b 3. c 4. g 5. a 6. f 7. d

Lesson 5 Global concerns in the business world SB Pages 66–67

In this lesson, students consider the field of business from a global perspective and discuss a variety of topics. The lesson starts with a series of discussion activities in which they share and discuss opinions. The second half of the lesson combines listening and discussion activities, including one in which students predict changes in the price of oil. To end the lesson, students research and present information about alternative sources of energy.

a
- With books closed, discuss the way both employees and employers have some concerns that are personal and limited to themselves and others that are more far-reaching in their scope. Illustrate the point by describing some real examples of a person who is concerned about his/her working conditions, job security and prospects, pension plan, etc., but also feels concerned about issues like the environment, fair trade with poorer nations, etc.
- Ask students to open their books and to look at the list of issues. Ask them to work alone numbering the issues from 1 to 10 (with 1 being the most important) from the point of view of an employee.

b
- Read aloud the example sentences. Then elicit ways in which the two sentences could be joined using a connector to mark contrast. For example, *I rate contract length as the most important issue while you put this as least important.*
- Organize students into pairs and have them compare their ratings with those of a classmate.

c
- Draw to students' attention the words and phrases in the box for expressing opinions and for marking contrast.
- Now organize students into pairs of pairs and have them share what they just discussed with their partners in groups of four. Encourage them to use the expressions in the box as they discuss their ideas.

d
- Ask students to look again at the list of issues in Exercise a. Have them say which issues they think are more restricted to a person's individual concerns and which issues have a wider scope.
- Read aloud the discussion questions. Then organize students into pairs or small groups and have them discuss the questions. Then open up the discussion for the whole group focusing on ways in which an individual employee can exert influence on the policy of the company he/she works for.

 e
CD T-44
- Tell students that they are going to hear a businessperson talking about a variety of issues that affect business.
- Ask students to listen to the audio straight through and to identify the specific industry that the speaker is referring to. Check the answer.

> **Answers**
> the clothing industry

 f
CD T-45
- Read aloud the list of issues and make sure that students understand the meaning of each term.
- Then ask students to listen to the audio again and to number the items in the order that they are mentioned by the speaker. Check answers.

> **Answers**
> 1. labor costs 2. outsourcing 3. marketing costs 4. raw materials 5. fashion trends
> 6. people's tastes 7. competition 8. inflation 9. production costs 10. pollution control

g
- Read aloud the discussion topic. Organize students into small groups and have them discuss the topic.
- Then open up the discussion for the whole group. Encourage students to refer to news items that they have seen or heard recently.

h (CD T-46)
- Tell students that they are going to hear some information about changes in the price of oil over the last few years. Ask students first to listen to the whole audio once through for the general idea.
- Then have students listen to the audio again and make notes about changes in the price of oil. Check answers.

> **Answers**
> mid-1990s - $11 a barrel, late 1990s - $25 a barrel, after September 2001 - $50 a barrel, 2005 - $72 a barrel

i
- Ask students to work alone converting the data they obtained from the audio into a line graph.
- Have students compare their graphs with those of the classmates.

j
- Draw to students' attention the expressions in the box. Elicit or point out that they all, with greater or lesser certainty, express predictions about the future.
- Organize students into small groups and have them discuss their predictions about the cost of oil over the next five years.

k
- Read aloud the types of energy in the box and ask students briefly to share what they know about these forms of energy. Discuss the fact that all of them are still considered to be alternative sources of energy.
- Then organize students into new groups of four and have each student choose one form of energy to research. Students conduct research and then report their findings to their own group outlining its advantages and disadvantages.

l
- After students have heard about the advantages and disadvantages of each type of energy, have them try to arrive at a consensus about the type of energy that they consider to be the most preferable.
- Invite each group to share its findings and opinions with the rest of the class. Then open up the topic for whole-class discussion.

Additional Activity Unit 5 - Lesson 5   page 86

Answers
1. 1. advocates 2. human 3. critics 4. living 5. inequalities 6. systems 7. effort 8. government 9. mechanisms 10. equality
2. Answers will vary.

Lesson 5

Lesson 6 Ethical trading

SB Pages 68–69

This lesson deals with the subject of ethical trading, a relatively recent concept in business. Students begin with discussion questions. They then read and complete a text about ethical trading and listen to check their answers. This is followed by another listening activity. Students then study a graph, read an article, and answer some questions about the growth of ethical trading. The grammatical focus of this lesson is the passive voice. The lesson ends with an exercise involving reported speech

a
- With books closed, elicit definitions of the word *ethics*. Students may come up with ideas such as "the principles of conduct governing an individual or a group" or "a set of moral principles or values". Alternatively, ask students to suggest synonyms for the word ethical, for example, *principled, right, fair, decent, just*.
- Ask students to open their books and have them read the discussion questions. Organize students into pairs or small groups and have them discuss the questions. Then open up the discussion for the whole group.

b
- First, ask students to look at the photograph. Ask: *What is this product? What do cosmetic products have to do with ethical trading?* Then read aloud the first sentence from the text.
- Then ask students to work alone or in pairs completing the rest of the text with the words from the box.

c CD T-47
- Ask students to listen to check their answers to the previous exercise.
- Then encourage students to share their reactions to what they read in the text.

> **Answers**
> 1. Ethical 2. beliefs 3. profitable 4. chemistry 5. testing 6. capital 7. investment 8. growth

d CD T-48
- Ask students to read through the two lists of companies. Ask them to say which ones they have heard of.
- Have students listen to the audio and match each ethical company with the larger company that bought it. Check and discuss answers.

> **Answers**
> 1. L'Oreal 2. Colgate 3. Hain Celestial 4. Unilever
> 5. Cadbury-Schweppes 6. Coca-cola 7. Danone

e
- Direct students' attention to the bar chart in **f**. Make sure that students understand exactly what information is shown in the graph.
- Organize students into pairs and have them discuss the growth of fair trading from 1998 through 2005. Elicit observation and comment.

f
- Set a time limit and have students skim through the article for the main ideas. Ask a few simple questions about the text to check students' understanding.
- Then have students read the questions. Ask them to read the article again and to answer the questions in their notebooks. Check answers.

> **Answers**
> 1. basic commodities such as coffee, sugar, cocoa 2. specialist shops and some supermarkets
> 3. 0.1% 4. workers' rights and environmental claims

g
- Briefly review the fact that the passive voice is often used in formal, scientific, and technical contexts for explaining a process, a phenomenon, a technique, a trend, etc.
- Have students work alone going through the article and underlining examples of the passive voice. Check answers.
- Then ask students to work in pairs discussing the use of the passive voice in the examples that they found.

> **Answers**
> was established, were faced, are involved, are paid, are stocked, can be found, must be taken, to be resolved, are produced, are sold, is hoped, are brought

h
- Briefly review the difference between direct quotation (i.e. the actual words that a person used) and reported speech. Remind students that in written English, direct speech is set inside quotation marks.
- Read aloud the example and ask students to identify the place in the text where the same information occurs but in reported speech (...ethical trading had taken ten years to really get going.). Then have students work alone or in pairs looking for more examples of reported speech in the text and "converting" each one back into the exact words that the speaker said.

> **Answers**
> "Ethical trading has taken ten years to really get going."
> "Research shows that 50% of people recognize the Fairtrade mark and it has huge potential for further growth."
> "Many people like the idea and they can buy the products at their local supermarket instead of going to a specialist wholefood supplier."
> "Retailers stock Fairtrade products because they are flying off the shelves."
> "The big increase in demand for Fairtrade and organic Easter eggs this year shows how mainstream they are becoming."

Additional Activity Unit 5 - Lesson 6   page 86

Answers
1. 1. During the 90s, many companies were put under pressure to ensure decent work conditions.
   2. Consumers' awareness of poor working conditions in developing countries was/has been raised.
   3. Some form of ethical sourcing policy has been adopted by many companies.
   4. Investments are screened according to a range of social and environmental criteria.
   5. Nowadays, ethical sourcing issues cannot be ignored.
2. Answers will vary.

Reading Resource 5B page 96

This reading is about corporate takeovers - why and how they happen. Students complete tasks focusing on general and specific understanding before completing vocabulary exercises.

Answers
A 1. Definitions and Terms 2. Benefits 3. Drawbacks
B 1. It can serve to reduce overcapacity in an industry. 2. The company can increase its market share. 3. The bidder first informs the board of the target company. 4. There is reduced competition and less choice for consumers.

Team Project 5

Prepare a report about future business trends SB Page 70

- Organize students into groups of four or five. Read aloud the instructions and make sure that students understand what they are to do.
- Spend some time discussing why it is important for businesses to be aware of future trends. Elicit ideas on this topic.
- Discuss with students how they might go about making initial contact with companies in their town / city.
- Have students prepare their reports. Encourage them to make their reports as full and informative as possible and to include any relevant visual aids such as diagrams, charts, graphs, etc. when they present their findings.

Review 5

SB page 76

Answer Key

A
1. Did you meet / had left / arrived 2. was looking / was just talking / wants
3. are going / are using / do not engage / do not waste 4. closed / helped

B
1. catch on 2. gets on 3. tune in 4. fed up 5. works out / is working out
6. turned out / is turning out

C
1. The secretary reminded the manager to sign the report. 2. Jackie apologized for missed the meeting the previous day. 3. The supervisor asked if anyone had phoned while he was out. 4. Simon suggested going out for lunch that day. 5. Manager ordered the report to be ready by three o' clock. 6. Janet asked if she could leave early that afternoon.

Unit 1 Additional Activities

Photocopiable

ACTIVITY 1.1

1 Match each term in the box with the correct definition.

| duties | experience | negotiable | qualifications | benefits |
| recruitment agency | candidate | counselor | salary | skills |

qualifications — proof that one has gained a certain level of knowledge or skill
_____ — fixed monthly payment received by employees of a company
_____ — tasks that employees are expected to perform as part of their jobs
_____ — a person who wants to be chosen for a job
_____ — able to be settled or changed through discussion
_____ — extra things that companies give to employees in addition to salaries
_____ — special abilities usually acquired through learning and practice
_____ — knowledge and skill acquired over time
_____ — an organization that matches applicants with vacant positions
_____ — a person who provides support and advice

2 In pairs, role-play a conversation in which a counselor gives advice to a person who is looking for a job.

ACTIVITY 1.2

1 Underline the correct spelling of each of the following words.

1. a. advertisment   b. advertisement   c. advertissement
2. a. acommodation   b. accomodation   c. accommodation
3. a. questionnaire   b. questionaire   c. questionairre
4. a. comittee   b. commitee   c. committee
5. a. necesarily   b. necessarily   c. nescessarily
6. a. responsability   b. responsebility   c. responsibility
7. a. commission   b. commision   c. comission

2 In pairs, test each other on the spellings of these words and other words that you find difficult to spell.

Additional Activities

Unit 1

ACTIVITY 1.3

1 Complete the phrasal verb with the correct preposition in each sentence.

1. If you leave something _____out_____, you don't include it.
2. Another way to say "to submit" is "to hand _____".
3. When you complete an application form, you fill it _____.
4. "Request" is a more formal way of saying "ask _____".
5. When you look _____ something, you consider it.
6. He didn't arrive early for his interview. In fact, he turned _____ twenty minutes late.
7. When you fill something _____, it becomes completely full.
8. They turned his application _____ - that is, they rejected it.
9. "Talk _____" is an informal way of saying "discuss".
10. If you replace someone temporarily, you fill _____ for them.

2 In pairs, write your own sample sentences to illustrate the meaning of each of the phrasal verbs above.

That section is optional. You can leave it out if you want.

ACTIVITY 1.4

1 Write each heading from the box in the correct space.

| Experience | Education | Skills | Personal characteristics | Extracurricular |

Things an interviewer will take into account and will want to know more about:

1. _____Personal characteristics_____ appearance, attitude, enthusiasm, general morale, etc.
2. _____ academic qualifications plus other relevant certification.
3. _____ communication skills, the ability to use current technology, and any foreign languages spoken.
4. _____ information about former and present employees, positions of responsibility held, and any promotions earned.
5. _____ a candidate's hobbies, sports, voluntary service, etc.

2 In pairs, role-play a job interview in which the interviewer asks a candidate for more information about the topics above.

Photocopiable

Additional Activities

Unit 1

ACTIVITY 1.5

1 Rewrite each sentence using a more formal register.

1. Well, here's my resume and a completed application form.
   I enclose my resume and a completed application form.

2. I think I'm pretty up to date with the latest computer software.
   _____

3. Anyway, e-mail me at this address or give me a call.
   _____

4. I like the sound of the Production Assistant job. I guess I could do that.
   _____

5. It would be really cool to work for a big company like yours.
   _____

6. After I left college, I took a special business course. That would be useful, right?
   _____

7. So, can we set up an interview some time soon?
   _____

2 In pairs, compare and discuss your answers.

ACTIVITY 1.6

1 Complete each sentence with the correct form of *make* or *do*.

1. Try not to worry during exams. The important thing is to _____*do*_____ your best.
2. If you want to speak with the director, you will have to _____ an appointment.
3. I demand to see the manger. I want to _____ a complaint.
4. I think you should stop wasting time and _____ some work for a change!
5. Don't blame yourself so much. Anyone can _____ a mistake.
6. It has been a pleasure to _____ business with you.
7. They have just _____ an amazing discovery.
8. Don't mention it. We're just _____ our job.

2 In pairs, make a list of expressions using *make* or *do*.

Unit 1   Photocopiable

Unit 2 Additional Activities

ACTIVITY 2.1

1 Match each sales term in the box with the correct definition.

| benefits | buying signal | close | features | money hours | prospect |

1. _____features_____: the attributes of a product or service that define it
2. _____: the value and advantages experienced by the customer
3. _____: a person or organization that may need or want to buy something
4. _____: the time in a salesperson's day when he/she can talk with prospects
5. _____: a sign from a prospect that indicates he/she wants to make a purchase
6. _____: when a salesperson asks a prospect to make a commitment to buy

2 In your notebook, write sample sentences illustrating how these terms above are used.

This model has some special new features.

ACTIVITY 2.2

1 Read the notes on how to set up an interview by telephone. Use them as the basis for a paragraph to be included in a guide for trainee salespeople. Illustrate steps using sequence expressions such as *first, next, then, after that,* and *finally*.

> **Setting up an interview by phone**
> Introduce yourself: talking to the right person?
> Check: convenient time to talk? is the person a prospective customer?
>   refer to brochure sent out previously
> Probe: is person a genuine prospect?
>   suggest meeting prospective customer
>   mention advantage of face-to-face meetings
> Ask: convenient time and place?
> Customer objections: reassure them – meeting is not a commitment
> Confirm arrangements: date, time of meeting

2 In pairs, role-play a telemarketing phone call in which a salesperson tries to set up a meeting with a prospective customer.

Photocopiable

Additional Activities

Unit 2

ACTIVITY 2.3

1 Write a description of the following pie chart, which shows the total retail sales for seven types of products in a large UK department store for 2006. Comment on the figures.

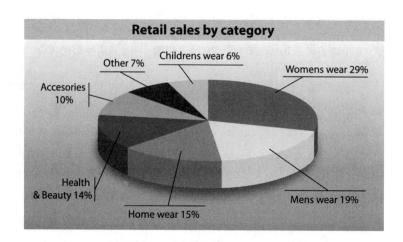

Retail sales by category: Other 7%, Childrens wear 6%, Womens wear 29%, Accesories 10%, Health & Beauty 14%, Home wear 15%, Mens wear 19%

2 In your notebook, draw a line graph, a pie chart, or a bar chart to illustrate the data in the following chart.

Best Selling Cars in the USA in 2006	2006 sales	2005 sales
#1. Ford F-Series pickup	555,953	615,057
#2. Chevrolet Silverado pickup	432,939	531,236
#3. Toyota Camry convertible, coupe and sedan	312,636	289,607
#4. Toyota Corolla sedan	275,072	245,981
#5. Honda Accord coupe and sedan	252,653	248,524

ACTIVITY 2.4

1 Read and complete the sentences with the correct prepositions.

1. Door-____to____-door selling is less common than it once was.
2. Mail-order buying _____ catalogs is still a popular way to shop.
3. In direct-mail selling, the approach to the customer is _____ mail.
4. Telemarketing involves sales solicitation _____ the telephone.
5. Many products are sold through paid programming _____ TV.

2 In your notebook, write examples of products or services that are (or were) typically sold via each of the sales methods mentioned above.

Additional Activities

Unit 2

ACTIVITY 2.5

1 Complete the text with the verbs in the box.

| Type | State | Include | Keep | Avoid | Save | Send |

Writing a Letter of Complaint

1. ___Include___ your name, address, and home and work telephone numbers.
2. _____ your letter if possible. If it is handwritten, make sure it is neat and easy to read.
3. _____ your letter brief and to the point. Mention all the relevant information about your purchase, including the date and place where it was bought and any information about the product such as serial or model numbers.
4. _____ exactly what you want done concerning the problem and say how long you are willing to wait to have it resolved. Be reasonable.
5. _____ all documents relating to the problem but be sure to send copies, not originals.
6. _____ using an angry, sarcastic, or threatening tone. The person who reads it was probably not responsible for the problem but they may well be able to help you to resolve it.
7. _____ a copy of your letter for your records.

2 Write a letter of complaint about a product or service following these guidelines.

ACTIVITY 2.6

1 Booksandstuff.com invites its customers to write reviews of books they have bought and enjoyed. In your notebook, write a review of the following book using the notes as a guide.

Title: *How to Sell*
Author: *Robert Ashton*
Publisher: *Hamilton-Ryce*
Book layout: *6 parts - each part divided into 8 to 12 sections*
Useful information: *qualities of a good salesperson*
Definitions of key terms: *lots of examples*
Reading difficulty: *language not difficult, information summarized clearly*
Honesty: *both positive and negative aspects of sales covered*
Recommendation: *Highly recommended*

2 In pairs, discuss the merits of books you have read in connection with your studies or work. Make recommendations about the best titles.

Unit 3 Additional Activities

ACTIVITY 3.1

1 Read the text and number the lines in the correct order.

___ was a growth in mass communication media, first, with newspapers and magazines and
___ systems of mass production and mass distribution of goods. This meant that, for most
_1_ Advertising is basically a form of selling. For thousands of years, individuals tried
___ companies, person-to-person selling was too slow and expensive. At the same time, there
___ could provide. The Industrial Revolution of the 18th and 19th centuries gave rise to
___ then, is selling through the paid space or time of various mass communication media.
___ to persuade others to buy the goods that they had produced or the services that they
___ then through radio and television. This made mass advertising possible. Advertising,

2 In your notebook, summarize the key ideas of the text in no more than fifty words.

3 Prepare a short report on one of the topics in the box as it relates to your country.

> The history of advertising   Major advertising agencies
> The story behind a successful recent advertising campaign

ACTIVITY 3.2

1 Complete the interview about Sunny Delight orange juice with appropriate questions.

1. *When was Sunny Delight first launched?*
   Sunny Delight was first launched in 1998.

2. _____
   It was marketed as a healthy fruit drink.

3. _____
   No, this was not true. In fact, it contained only 5% juice plus lots of sugar, water, vegetable oil, thickeners, flavorings, and colorings.

4. _____
   The product was taken off the market.

2 In pairs, role-play an interview in which a former employee of the company that produced Sunny Delight explains the story of the product.

Unit 3   Photocopiable

Additional Activities

Unit 3

ACTIVITY 3.3

1 Complete each space in the text with a word from the box.

| attitudes | purchasing | analysis | population | relationship | brand |
| customer | | achieve | | | |

Sellers aim to give the (1) ___customer___ what he or she wants. Finding out what the customer wants is what marketing research tries to (2) _____. Some people define marketing research as the scientific (3) _____ of marketing problems. It studies people as buyers and sellers, examining their habits, (4) _____, preferences, dislikes, and their (5) _____ power. Marketing research often focuses on specific segments of the (6) _____, such as teenagers, high-income groups, or senior citizens. Marketing research also studies distribution systems, pricing, promotion, product design, packaging, (7) _____ names—in fact, almost every aspect of the (8) _____ between seller and buyer.

2 In your notebook, write a definition for each of the words in the box.

customer = a person or organization that buys goods or services from a store, a business, etc.

ACTIVITY 3.4

1 Complete each sentence with a word related to the word given in capitals.

1. Most software nowadays is very easy to ___install___. — INSTALLATION
2. We have seen substantial _____ in sales over the last year. — GROW
3. That product is not on sale yet. It is still in _____. — DEVELOP
4. I am focusing on this one campaign to the _____ of all others. — EXCLUDE
5. An _____ is a very effective way of selling a product. — ENDORSE
6. Personally, I don't find his arguments very _____. — CONVINCE
7. There is a growing feeling of _____ about the campaign. — ANTICIPATE
8. We didn't _____ that product to sell as well as it did. — EXPECTATION
9. I don't _____ of that company's marketing methods. — APPROVAL
10. The most striking thing about that ad was its _____. — ORIGINAL

2 In pairs, role-play a conversation between an expert and a layperson about marketing.

Additional Activities

Unit 3

ACTIVITY 3.5

1 Look at the expressions in the box. Sort them into formal and informal expressions and write them in the corresponding columns.

> meeting   just to let you know   real sorry   would like to apologize   unable to attend
> something else on   give you a buzz   previous commitment   contact you
> see you later   unfortunately   inform you   can't make it   get together

FORMAL	INFORMAL

2 Imagine you work in the marketing department of a company. You are unable to attend an important meeting. In your notebook, write a note of apology to the Marketing Manager. Use appropriate phrases from the list above.

ACTIVITY 3.6

1 Match the two halves of the sentences.

1. A counterfeit is an imitation made deliberately   _c_
2. Apart from forged currency or documents, counterfeits   ___
3. In the USA, the FBI estimates that American companies lose   ___
4. According to the European Commission, counterfeit goods   ___
5. Expensive or desirable brands   ___
6. The popularity of designer jeans such as Jordache in the late 1970s   ___

a. cause 100,000 job losses in Europe each year.
b. produced a flood of illegal copies.
c. to falsely represent its content or its origins.
d. up to $250 billion a year due to counterfeit goods.
e. have become popular among counterfeiters.
f. can also be clothes, software, pharmaceuticals, etc.

2 In pairs, role-play a conversation between an expert and a layperson about the problem of pirated/counterfeited goods.

Unit 4 Additional Activities

ACTIVITY 4.1

1 Read the tips about managing money and cutting expenses while at college. Match each heading in the box with the correct tip.

> Work while at college   Used books   "Extra" expenses   Consider a roommate

1. _"Extra" expenses_ Keep your phone bill down by avoiding expensive options (call waiting, voice messaging, etc.) and by using e-mail. Go to matinees instead of evening shows.
2. _____ Save money by acquiring used books at bookstores or from other students. When you are finished, you may be able to sell them to someone else.
3. _____ Sharing accommodation can reduce monthly living expenses.
4. _____ A part-time job can provide extra spending money as well valuable work experience.

ACTIVITY 4.2

1 Match the two halves of the sentences.

1. Financial institutions are companies that deal in money   _d_
2. The financial institution that most people know best is   ___
3. A bank is an establishment in which individuals,   ___
4. From these deposits the bank makes   ___
5. The interest earned on these loans is a chief source   ___
6. Deposits represent the largest source of commercial bank income—   ___
7. Checking accounts are the means by which most people and institutions   ___

a. of income for the bank.
b. usually more than 80 percent.
c. businesses, government agencies, and even other banks deposit money.
d. or money equivalents, such as stocks and bonds.
e. pay their bills.
f. loans to individuals, businesses, government agencies, and other banks.
g. the commercial bank.

2 Prepare a short oral report about banks and the banking system in your country.

Photocopiable

Unit 4

Additional Activities

Unit 4

ACTIVITY 4.3

1 Using the following notes plus your own ideas, write a letter in your notebook offering advice to a friend who is trying to reduce expenses in his/her small hotel business.

> *Review expenses regularly:* ask for suggestions from staff on how to cut costs
> *Save energy:* use energy-saving light bulbs, timers on hall lights, pool cover at night, turn off TVs when not in use
> *Develop awareness among staff:* environmental value of energy saving
> *Check suppliers' prices:* change suppliers if there is a better deal, same with telephone companies
> *Insurance:* very important to shop around
> *Communication:* use e-mail rather than postal service whenever possible, set up on-line booking facilities, put catalog online

2 In pairs, role-play a conversation in which two friends compare and discuss problems they have had in managing expenses.

ACTIVITY 4.4

1 Complete each space in the text with a word from the box.

demand	inelastic	elastic	economic	falls
inverse	percentage		increases	direct
economists		income		price

Demand for a product is affected by a range of variables. Two key variables are the (1) ___*price*___ of the product, and consumers' (2) _____. According to (3) _____ theory, there is normally an (4) _____ relationship between the price of a product and the quantity demanded of that product. As price (5) _____, the quantity demanded increases. There is also normally a (6) _____ relationship between consumers' income and the quantity demanded at any given price; i.e. as consumers' income increases, demand (7) _____. The (8) _____ for some products is very responsive to changes in price or in consumers' income. A certain (9) _____ change in price or income leads to a greater percentage change in the quantity demanded. (10) _____ describe such products as having (11) _____ demand. The demand for some other products is much less responsive to changes in price or income. These products are said to have (12) _____ demand.

2 In pairs, role-play a conversation between an expert and a layperson about the demand elasticity.

Additional Activities

Unit 4

ACTIVITY 4.5

1 Read the text and number the lines in the correct order.

___ can borrow it, and in doing so they issue certificates of debt. These certificates are called
___ obtain money through taxation or through borrowing. When a government borrows, it
___ them. A person who buys a bond expects, over time, to recover the principal (the amount
___ money). Corporations also have two means of raising money (apart from profits). They
_1_ Governments and corporations need money in order to operate. Governments can
___ bonds. As with government bonds, interest is paid to the buyer. The second way for a
___ issues bonds, or certificates of debt. These certificates pay interest to the people that buy
___ company to raise money is to issue stocks, which represent ownership in the corporation.
___ of the loan) plus the interest (the fee the government pays the lender for the use of the

2 In your notebook, summarize the key ideas of the text in no more than fifty words.

ACTIVITY 4.6

1 Complete each sentence with a word related to the word given in capitals.

1. The ___*origins*___ of stock trading go back to the 13th century.   ORIGINAL
2. Stock trading has _____ tremendously in recent years.   EVOLUTION
3. Technology has allowed the stock market to grow _____.   TREMENDOUS
4. Society has _____ this growth.   ENCOURAGEMENT
5. Before, only those who could afford _____ stockbrokers could trade.   EXPENSE
6. Now, anyone wanting to _____ in the stock market can do so.   PARTICIPATION
7. The Internet has _____ the development of on-line trading.   PERMISSION
8. Trading can be done through _____ devices like handheld computers.   MOBILITY
9. Within seconds of an order being made, the _____ takes place.   TRANSACT
10. Day trading is now a _____ thanks to these advances in technology.   POSSIBLE

2 Prepare a short written report on one of the topics in the box as it relates to your country.

```
Types of transactions used        Places where information about stocks is published
   The stock exchange             Technology used to perform transactions
```

Photocopiable   Unit 4 83

Unit 5 Additional Activities

ACTIVITY 5.1

1 Read the advice for foreigners doing business in Japan. Complete each item with Do or Don't.

1. ___Do___ try to be introduced through a trusted customer, client, employer, etc.
2. _____ arrive late.
3. _____ bow slightly when introduced to someone or when leaving a meeting.
4. _____ study a person's name card/business card carefully and respectfully.
5. _____ write anything on someone's business card.
6. _____ toss your business card across a table to someone.
7. _____ provide a dinner meeting at some point.
8. _____ press too hard for a commitment or be too aggressive when closing a deal.
9. _____ follow up a meeting with a thank you fax, e-mail, or letter.

2 In pairs, write a list of advice for foreigners doing business in your country.

ACTIVITY 5.2

1 Match the problems with the solutions.

1. What caused me a lot of stress at first was that I was constantly working to meet my boss' impossible deadlines. ___b___
2. E-mail is wonderful but it can also cause stress. People at my office used to send e-mails about unimportant things. I was afraid to delete them unread in case I missed something. _____
3. For me, the most stressful thing was giving a presentation in front of a group of colleagues. The first time I did this, I was really stressed out. _____
4. At my first job, the manager liked to intimidate people during performance appraisals. This made me very nervous about the whole thing. In fact, appraisals still make me feel apprehensive. _____

a. Then I took a couple of workshops on effective presentation giving and now I feel better about it.
b. Now I understand how he thinks and I anticipate what has to be done "very quickly" and what can be done just "quickly". Prioritizing like this helps me cope.
c. Now I try to analyze my own performance and make notes about good and not so good points. Being prepared in this way helps a lot.
d. So, I sent an e-mail to all my colleagues asking them to clarify in the subject line what an e-mail is about and what level of priority it has. I found that this helped a lot.

2 In pairs, brainstorm and make a list of other things that can cause stress in the workplace. Discuss your ideas.

Additional Activities

Unit 5

ACTIVITY 5.3

1 Read the text and number the lines in the correct order.

___ how to perform a task. Instead, it focuses on communicating the results that it
___ from those business relationships in which the buyer retains control of the
___ of one of its business processes to an outside supplier. The key aspect in this
___ and what can make it such a challenging and sometimes painful process – is this
_1_ In essence, outsourcing takes place when an organization transfers ownership
___ wants to buy. The process of accomplishing those results is left to the supplier.
___ transfer of ownership. In outsourcing, the buyer does not instruct the supplier
___ process, i.e. telling the supplier how to do the work. What defines outsourcing—
___ definition is the transfer of control. In this definition, outsourcing is different

2 In pairs, role-play a conversation between an expert and a layperson about outsourcing.

ACTIVITY 5.4

1 Match the two halves of the sentences.

1. Corporate fraud is an undeniable fact of business life   _e_
2. New technologies such as the Internet   ___
3. Once suspected or discovered, investigating fraud   ___
4. There is no doubt that fraud is best prevented,   ___
5. There is no completely foolproof method of preventing fraud,   ___
6. Special techniques are used to pro-actively   ___
7. Other techniques are used to further investigate so that   ___

a. although there are a range of effective fraud prevention techniques.
b. have increased the opportunities for fraud to be committed.
c. is a specialist task requiring experience and technical skill.
d. fraud incidents are satisfactorily resolved.
e. affecting businesses large and small.
f. test for fraud profiles.
g. rather than dealt with after the fact.

Photocopiable

Additional Activities
Unit 5

ACTIVITY 5.5

1 Complete each space in the text with a word from the box.

| living | inequalities | systems | effort | equality |
| government | mechanisms | advocates | human | critics |

(1) __Advocates__ of capitalism consider economic freedom to be a basic (2) _____ liberty. However, (3) _____ of the market system claim that it does not provide an equally high standard of (4) _____ for everyone. This is undeniably true. Under capitalism, there are (5) _____ of wealth, though much less so than under other (6) _____. To a large degree, success in a free market depends on individual (7) _____ and ability, qualities that are distributed unevenly among human beings. The only way to achieve the goal of complete equality of wealth is by the use of some sort of (8) _____ force. The market economy has no (9) _____ of coercion available to it and it does not guarantee equal wealth for all. It tries to maintain liberty and (10) _____ under law for all participants.

2 In pairs or small groups, discuss the positive and negative aspects of free market economies.

ACTIVITY 5.6

1 Write passive voice sentences from the prompts.

1. during the 90s / many companies / put / under pressure / ensure / decent work conditions
   During the 90s, many companies were put under pressure to ensure decent work conditions.

2. consumers' awareness / poor working conditions / in developing countries / raise
   _____

3. some form of ethical sourcing policy / adopted / many companies
   _____

4. investments / screen / according to / a range of social and environmental criteria
   _____

5. nowadays / ethical sourcing issues / cannot / ignore
   _____

2 Research and prepare a short report about ethical trading initiatives in your country.

Reading Resources
Unit 1
Photocopiable

Reading A

a Answer these questions.

1. Do you know anyone who has used the Internet to look for a job?
2. Are there any job Web sites specifically for your city?

b Read and number the paragraphs in the correct order.

____ They felt a bit disheartened and even thought about calling it a day. But in the end they decided to make a go of it. "After all," explained Alan, "we were just sort of dragging our heels and didn't have a lot else to do." So they got down to work and got their Web site off the ground last April.

____ Dave Rosen and Alan Bailey graduated two years ago after taking courses in business at their hometown university. They were two of the best students in their year and they passed their exams with flying colors. One might think that it would be easy for graduates like these to find a job. But when Dave and Alan started looking for work, they found it an uphill struggle because their city had no coordinated job search center.

____ Soon after launching the site, they were pleasantly surprised to receive lots of enquiries about advertising. So they designed attractive advertising spaces and they sold like hot cakes. In the eyes of many people, Dave and Alan have it made. They provide a great service for other jobseekers and, by using their initiative, they have turned a job hunt into a job.

____ Using their knowledge of business and their computer skills, they decided to take matters into their own hands. They spent hours walking around the city collecting as much information as possible about vacant positions. "At first we just had a big mountain of stuff but it wasn't organized," said Dave. "My room was a bit of a mess with hundreds of papers all over the floor!"

c Find idiomatic expressions in the text that mean the same as the following phrases.

1. with great success: _with flying colors_
2. a big mess: _____
3. quickly and in large quantities: _____
4. take the initiative: _____
5. giving up: _____
6. have everything one needs: _____
7. try to make a success of something: _____
8. up and running: _____
9. very difficult: _____
10. doing nothing: _____

Reading Resources

Unit 1 — Photocopiable

Reading B

a Read and complete the text with words from the box. There are two extra words.

| fashion | prosper | traditional | manufacturing | material | asset | firing |
| managers | maximize | | objectives | contact | economy | |

In (1) __traditional__ economic theory, the term human resources referred simply to labor, one of the three factors of production. Nowadays, human resources (HR) is the people that staff and operate an organization as contrasted with its financial and (2) _____ resources. Human resources is also the organizational function dealing with people and issues related to people such as: hiring and (3) _____, compensation, training, performance, organizational development, health and safety, benefits, motivation, communication, etc. HR (4) _____ are obliged and expected to carry out these activities in an effective, legal, fair, and consistent (5) _____. The objective of human resources is to (6) _____ the return on investment from an organization's human capital. HR management aims to improve individuals' productive contribution to an organization while simultaneously trying to achieve other societal and individual (7) _____. Sometimes in large companies there is not a lot of direct (8) _____ between top management and the majority of employees. The HR department plays a crucial liaison role between a company and it's most precious (9) _____ — its employees. Today, human resources is a vital part of a company. A company that does not attend to its human resources issues will not (10) _____.

b Find words in the text that mean the same as the following expressions.

1. at the same time   __simultaneously__
2. valuable   _____
3. conventional   _____
4. vital   _____
5. impartial   _____
6. make a profit   _____

c Summarize the main ideas of the text in approximately 100 words.

Reading Resources

Unit 2　　　　　　　　　　　　　　　　　　　　Photocopiable

Reading A

a Read the text. Then complete the notes with the correct information from the article.

> In July 1977, a boycott was begun in the United States against the Swiss-based Nestlé corporation. The boycott—still in effect—soon spread to other countries, particularly in Europe. Boycotters expressed concern about the company's marketing of powdered baby milk, particularly in less developed countries. Campaigners claim that by promoting the use of powdered formula instead of a mother's own milk, Nestlé has contributed to the unnecessary death and suffering of babies, especially those living in poor economic conditions.
>
> Greenpeace, Friends of the Earth, and People and Planet are the organizations behind the Stop Esso campaign, a boycott of the oil company Esso (known as ExxonMobil in the USA). These organizations claim that Esso is harming the environment by not investing in renewable sources of energy, by denying the existence of global warming, and by undermining the Kyoto Protocol.
>
> In September 2005, the Jyllands-Posten, a Danish newspaper, printed some cartoons that deeply offended many Muslims. In early 2006, there were protests—some of them violent—in many countries followed by a boycott of all Danish goods. The company most affected was Arla, which sells dairy products and which is Denmark's biggest Middle East exporter. The boycott also affected other companies like Bang & Olufsen and Lego.

Target of Boycott	Reasons for Boycott
1. 2. 3.	

b Read the text again. Then read the sentences and mark them True or False.

1. Nestlé markets powdered baby milk in less developed countries.　　　<u>True</u>　　False
2. The Danish company most affected by the boycott was Bang & Olufsen.　　True　　False
3. Some campaigners claim that Esso does not support the Kyoto Protocol.　　True　　False
4. The largest Danish exporter to the Middle East is Arla.　　True　　False
5. The boycott against Nestlé started in Europe.　　True　　False

c In your notebook, write sentences about the boycotts using phrases that express cause and effect. Use the expressions it the box.

to introduce a cause	because owing to	because of since	due to as	as a result of
to introduce an effect	so　　therefore	with the result that	resulting in	consequently

Reading Resources

Unit 2

Photocopiable

Reading B

a Answer the questions.

1. What consumer protection agencies exist in your country?
2. What services do they offer to the general public?

b Read the article. Match each phrase in the box with the correct paragraph.

Product labels and packaging	Questionable selling practices
There have been cases of advertising	Consumerism, consumer issues
The products that are the most controlled	

1. _Consumerism, consumer issues_, and consumer protection are largely 20th-century concepts. Nowadays, people want assurances that what is sold to the public is of good quality. Buyers today are protected by consumer protection laws that regulate the methods and standards of manufacturers, advertisers, and sellers. These laws cover manufacturing and design, labeling and packaging, advertising, and selling methods.

2. _____ by laws are food and drugs. Other products are controlled by various standards institutions. The best known of these in the United States is the American National Standards Institute.

3. _____ can be informative or be misleading. For most products, there are minimum labeling and packaging standards. Food and drugs are the most strictly regulated products.

4. _____ that presents misleading, inaccurate, or untruthful claims about products. In the United States, the Federal Trade Commission has the power to stop advertising that is considered misleading.

5. _____ are hard to regulate and control. Sometimes people feel pressured into making a purchase that they do not really want. In some countries, the law provides for a "cooling off" period in case the buyer has a change of heart. One rule that is enforced universally is the one that says that a product must be sold at its advertised price.

c Read the sentences. Check ✓ the ones that are true.

1. The Federal Trade Commission can stop an advertisement that is inaccurate.   ✓
2. As a concept, consumer protection goes back hundreds of years.   ____
3. Consumer protection laws regulate how things are made, advertised, and sold.   ____
4. There are strict labeling and packaging standards for food and drugs.   ____
5. In all countries, the law allows for a "cooling off" period.   ____

Reading Resources
Unit 3
Photocopiable

Reading A

a Skim through the text and select the best heading from the options in the box.

| Marketing in the 21st Century | Marketing Then and Now |
| Early Concepts in Marketing | Current Trends in Marketing |

b Scan the text to find the answers to the questions below.

Around 1910, the term marketing was added to the familiar terms distribution, trade, and commerce. Two of the people who were instrumental in initially stating this concept were Ralph Starr Butler and Arch W. Shaw. Shaw distinguished three basic operations in business: production, distribution, and administration. Recalling Bohm-Bawerk's concept that business is concerned with motion of one sort or another, Shaw conceived marketing as "matter in motion".

During the ten years following 1920, principles of marketing were first presented in book form, building upon foundations laid previously. Scattered concepts and tentative generalizations were integrated and much new material was incorporated into contemporary thinking. Paul W. Ivey was the first to actually use the title *Principles of Marketing*. During the 1920s, many "principles" books were published, the most important of which were by Paul D. Converse, Walter C. Weidler, Fred E. Clark, Theodore N. Beckman, and Harold H. Maynard. Clark defined marketing as "those efforts which effect transfer in the ownership of goods" while Converse, in *Marketing Methods and Policies,* made an early distinction between the marketing activities that relate to an individual firm and the marketing functions that pervade marketing in general.

A tendency observed during the 1930s was the simplification of theoretical writings on marketing with a view to their use for elementary academic purposes. During this time, marketing grew as an academic discipline.

1. When were marketing principles presented in book form for the first time?   *1920s*
2. Who thought of the concept that business is about motion?   _____
3. Who was the first person to publish a book called *Principles of Marketing?*   _____
4. When did marketing develop as a field of academic study?   _____
5. Who wrote a book called *Marketing Methods and Policies?*   _____

c Complete each space in the definition with a word related to the word in parentheses.

"Marketing is the (1) ___*performance*___ (perform) of business activities that (2) _____ (direction) the flow of goods and service from (3) _____ (production) to consumers or users in order to (4) _____ (satisfaction) consumers and accomplish the firms objectives." *(McCarthy)*

Reading Resources

Unit 3

Photocopiable

Reading B

a Answer these questions.

1. What do you know about Benetton and its advertising campaigns?
2. Do you think advertising should be a medium for social comment?

b Read the text quickly for the general ideas and match each heading in the box with the correct paragraph. There are two extra headings.

The Products	The Company	Controversy
The Creative Director	Consequences	The Customers

1. _____The Company_____: Benetton is a world famous clothing brand, named for the four Benetton siblings who founded the company in 1965. The brand is well known for its colorful clothes — especially sweaters — and also for the original and, in recent times, controversial images used in its advertising.

2. _____: Italian photographer Oliviero Toscani joined Benetton in 1982 and was granted a lot of artistic freedom by management. Rather than advertise specific products made by the company, most of Toscani's campaigns were institutional ads for the brand. They consisted of a striking photograph and the only text was the caption "United Colors of Benetton".

3. _____: Toscani's ads were frequently criticized for being sensational. Some of the most controversial images were of a man on his deathbed dying from AIDS, of an unwashed newborn baby with its umbilical cord still attached, of a priest and nun about to kiss each other on the mouth, of a black woman nursing a white baby, and of the blood-stained uniform of a soldier who died fighting in Bosnia-Herzegovina.

4. _____: In 2000, Toscani left Benetton after being with the company for 18 years. It had become clear that Toscani's controversial advertising campaigns were costing the company money. In February of that year, Sears Roebuck & Co. dropped Benetton's USA line in response to a Toscani ad campaign that featured inmates on death row. Benetton merchandise had been expected to generate $100 million in sales in its first year with Sears.

c Read the text again. Read the sentences and circle True or False.

1. The Benetton company was founded in 1982.   True   False
2. Benetton's most famous products are its colorful sweaters.   True   False
3. Oliviero Toscani was one of the founders of Benetton.   True   False
4. The Sears partnership generated $100 million in sales in its first year.   True   False
5. Some of Benetton's advertisements focused on the issue of AIDS.   True   False

d Summarize the main ideas of the text in approximately 100 words.

Reading Resources
Unit 4   Photocopiable

Reading A

a Read the article and answer the questions according to the information in the text.

> The U.S. commercial banking industry has undergone a series of important transformations in the last two or three decades. Since the 1980s, banks have increased the scope and <u>scale</u> of their activities and, through mergers and takeovers, several banks have become very large institutions with a nationwide presence. Thus, one of the main changes in the structure of the banking industry has been a movement toward <u>consolidation</u>.
>
> Innovations in communication have made the U.S. economy much more integrated nationally. This <u>trend</u> towards having national as opposed to regional operations is clear to see in the retail sector and this has consequences for the banking sector. A large <u>portion</u> of the banks' activities, such as providing checking accounts and other payment instruments, is essentially retail in nature and thus subject to the same market pressure to become national.
>
> Also, some of the banks' <u>chief</u> customers are retailer businesses, which, having acquired national presence themselves, are now more likely to benefit from an association with a bank that is also operating nationwide. In this way, the <u>natural</u> reaction of banks has been to move toward consolidation.

1. How have certain U.S. banks grown into large institutions?
   _____

2. According to the text, what has caused the U.S. economy to be more integrated?
   _____

3. Why is it significant that a large number of banking activities are retail in nature?
   _____

b The following words are underlined in the reading. In each case, underline the expression that is not a synonym in this context.

1. scale =   a. size   b. degree   c. ascent   d. extent
2. consolidation = a. strengthening   b. dividing   c. making secure   d. combining
3. trend =   a. movement   b. tendency   c. shift   d. look
4. portion =   a. part   b. ration   c. percentage   d. share
5. chief =   a. principal   b. main   c. leader   d. leading
6. natural =   a. relaxed   b. expected   c. understandable d. normal

c Summarize the main ideas of the text in approximately 100 words.

d Write a report about the products / services that banks offer nowadays that they did not offer ten years ago.

Reading Resource

Unit 4

Photocopiable

Reading B

a Look at the graphs showing information about debts, overdrafts, and savings. Read the statements and write True or False.

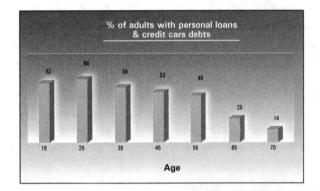
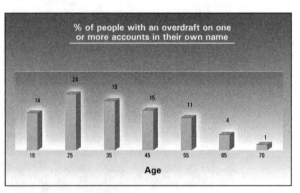
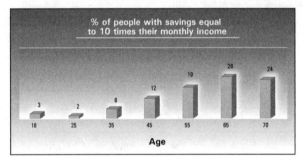

(Source: FSA)

1. More 35-year-olds than 45-year-olds have an overdraft on more than one account.   _____True_____
2. Only 2% of 25-year-olds have savings that are ten times their monthly income.   _____
3. 66% of 18-year-olds have personal loans and credit card debts.   _____
4. More 70-year-olds than 65-year-olds have savings 10 times their monthly income.   _____

b Look at the graphs again and answer the questions.

1. What overall patterns do you notice in the three graphs?
   _____

2. Which age group has the most savings in relation to monthly income?
   _____

3. What percentage of people aged 55 have personal loans and credit card debts?
   _____

Reading Resources
Unit 5
Photocopiable

Reading A

a Read the text. Then complete the sentences with the correct names.

> According to *Forbes* magazine, Microsoft co-founder and chairman Bill Gates is the richest person in the world and has been since 1995. Recent estimates calculate his net worth to be around $56 billion. Born in Seattle, Washington in 1955, Gates founded Microsoft with Paul Allen in 1975 and Gates is still its largest individual shareholder, holding more than 8% of the common stock. For the past thirty years, Gates has been one of the most famous and most recognized entrepreneurs in the world of computer technology. In recent years, Gates has become involved in various philanthropic projects.
>
> Now in second place behind Bill Gates on *Forbes'* list of the richest people in the world, is Mexican entrepreneur Carlos Slim, who was born in Mexico City in 1940. His fortune, which is estimated to be around US$53.1 billion, comes from his very strong position in the telecommunications industry in Mexico and in the whole of Latin America. He controls the Telmex, Telcel, and America Movil companies which are run on a day-to-day basis by his sons.
>
> Though not in the same mega-billionaire league as Gates and Slim, flamboyant global entrepreneur Sir Richard Branson is certainly as well-known - if not more so - to the general public. Born in 1950 in Surrey, England, Branson is best known for the Virgin brand that now comprises over 200 companies. He started in business when he was only 16 by publishing a magazine called *Student*. He then went on to set up a mail-order business selling records and this developed into a chain of record stores and a record label. The Virgin brand grew substantially in the 1980s with the launch of Virgin Atlantic Airways.

1. _____Gates_____ was born in the USA.
2. _____ has been involved in the music industry.
3. _____ is a philanthropist.
4. _____ has many business interests in Latin America.
5. _____ started in business when he was very young.
6. _____ was born in Mexico.

b Read the text again. Read the sentences and write True or False.

1. Branson, Gates, and Slim all have about the same net worth.   _____False_____
2. Richard Branson's first business ventures were in the 1970s.   _____
3. More than 200 companies make up the Virgin brand.   _____
4. Bill Gates founded Microsoft on his own.   _____
5. Carlos Slim no longer runs his companies day by day.   _____
6. The Microsoft company is over thirty years old.   _____

Additional Activities   Unit 5   95

Reading Resource

Unit 5

Photocopiable

Reading B

a Skim through the text and label each paragraph with an appropriate heading from the box. There are three extra headings.

| Legalities | Benefits | Financing a Takeover |
| Drawbacks | Reverse Takeovers | Definitions and Terms |

_____ In business, a takeover is when one company (called the acquirer or the bidder) buys another company (called the target). When a bidder makes an offer for another company, it usually informs the board of the target company first. If the board believes that the offer would be advantageous for its shareholders, they recommend that the shareholders accept the offer. A takeover is called a hostile takeover when the board rejects an offer but the bidder continues to pursue it or when the bidder makes an offer without previously informing the board.

_____ As with most business decisions, there are, potentially, both advantages and disadvantages in taking over another company. One positive benefit of a takeover can be an increase in sales and/or revenue for the acquiring company. Highly profitable companies often become the targets of takeover bids. Sometimes the reason for a takeover is because a company wants to venture into new businesses and markets. A takeover can enable a company to enlarge its portfolio of brands. This, in turn, can help a company to increase its market share. Related to this point is the fact that a takeover can serve to decrease the competition facing the acquiring company. Takeovers can sometimes serve to reduce overcapacity in an industry. In this way, takeovers have a streamlining, rationalizing effect.

_____ On the negative side, takeovers can produce oligopoly markets which results in reduced competition and less choice for consumers. Takeovers almost always bring with them the increased likelihood of price increases and redundancies. Takeovers can sometimes be beset by problems stemming from clashes between disparate cultures in the target company and the acquiring company. An acquiring company can sometimes face hidden liabilities within the target company that were not apparent at the time of the takeover.

b Read the text again, more carefully this time, and answer the questions.

1. How can a takeover have a streamlining effect on an industry?
   _____

2. What is one possible consequence when a company enlarges its portfolio of brands?
   _____

3. What is usually the first step in a non-hostile takeover?
   _____

4. What happens if takeovers produce oligopoly markets?
   _____

Writing Resources
Unit 1 — Photocopiable

Writing Resource 1A
Writing a job advertisement

Situation

You work in a Human Resources department. You have been asked to write an advertisement for a position that has recently become available.

Preparation

Choose ONE of the following positions to advertise.
- secretary at a university
- accounting assistant in a travel agency
- sales representative for a shoe company

Writing

A Select your position and brainstorm a list of what the job involves. Then start to arrange your ideas in some sort of logical order.

Ideas	Logical Sequence
_____	_____
_____	_____
_____	_____
_____	_____
_____	_____

B Now start to compose sentences outlining in detail the duties and responsibilities that the job involves, and the qualifications, skills, and experience that are required for the job. Use vocabulary and phrases typically found in job advertisements. For example, *Accountant required for...* or *Shoe manufacturer requires...*

Use the passive voice to explain procedures. For example, *On-the-job training is provided.* Use modals to explain requirements. For example, *Candidates should hold a diploma in sales. The successful candidate must enjoy working in a team.*

C Write a first draft of your advertisement. Check it and make corrections before writing out a final version.

> **Tips**
> - Use a formal style. Do not use contractions or colloquial expressions.
> - Abbreviated expressions are acceptable as long as they are standard abbreviations commonly used and understood in this field of work.

Writing Resources

Unit 1

Photocopiable

Writing Resource 1B

Writing a cover letter

Situation

You want to apply for a job and you have to write a cover letter to accompany your job application.

Preparation

Choose ONE of the following jobs to apply for:
- public relations officer for a TV company
- production assistant at a software company
- graphic designer in a publishing house

Writing

A Select your job and brainstorm a list of reasons why you think you are a suitable candidate for the position. Then start to arrange your ideas in a logical sequence.

Ideas	Logical Sequence
_____	_____
_____	_____
_____	_____
_____	_____
_____	_____

B Now start to compose sentences that will convince someone in human resources that they should call you for interview. Mention your availability for interview.

C Write a first draft of your cover letter. Check it and make corrections before writing out a final version.

Tips
■ Write in a formal register. Do not use contractions or colloquial expressions. ■ Some specialized technical language is acceptable since your cover letter will, at some point, be read by people with knowledge of your chosen field.

Writing Resources
Unit 2

Photocopiable

Writing Resource 2A
Writing a report about recent sales trends

Situation

You work for a consultancy firm that provides detailed information about different aspects of sales in various markets. You have been asked to prepare a report.

Preparation

Choose ONE of the following products:
- flat-screen TVs
- lactose-free milk and dairy products
- cell phones for children
- bottled drinking water

Writing

A Decide which product to write about. Look for information about sales trends and phenomena in your chosen product and make notes.

Sales Trends

_____   _____
_____   _____
_____   _____
_____   _____
_____   _____

B Now start to compose sentences outlining changes in the sales of your chosen product. Include information not just about overall figures but also relevant details about how the numbers break down, for example, over different geographical regions, over different sectors of society, between male and female users, between users of different age groups, etc.

Include your own observations about these phenomena and make predictions for what you think sales will be in the future. Along with your findings, present any relevant data in graphical form such as charts and graphs.

C Write a first draft of your report. Check it and make corrections before writing out a final version.

Tips
▪ Write in a formal register. Do not use contractions or colloquial expressions.
▪ You can include technical language in your report because it will be read by people who are knowledgeable in this field.

Writing Resources

Unit 2

Photocopiable

Writing Resource 2B
Writing a formal letter of complaint

Situation

You recently bought a product or received a service with which you are not satisfied. You wish to write a letter of complaint to the Customer Services department of the company you dealt with.

Preparation

Choose ONE of the following problems:
- Your bill for gas, water, electricity, etc. is four times the amount you expected. You believe the utility company has overcharged you.
- You bought a microwave oven but it only works if you set it to "one minute".
- You took your car to be serviced but now your car runs worse than it did before you took it to the agency.
- You bought a product for removing stains from clothes but, instead of removing the stains, it makes them worse.

Writing

A Decide which product or service to write about and make preliminary notes about the content of your letter.

Product: _____

Notes:

_____   _____
_____   _____
_____   _____
_____   _____

B Now start to compose sentences. Be sure to state the problem clearly, provide relevant details about when and where the product or service was purchased, and make clear what action you expect to be taken.

C Arrange your letter according to standard conventions of format and layout. At the start of your letter, include the relevant addresses, the date, and an appropriate salutation. End with a suitable signing off phrase, your name, and your signature.

D Write a first draft of your letter. Check it and make corrections before writing out a final version.

Tips
■ Write in a formal register. Do not use contractions or colloquial expressions. ■ The tone of your letter should be firm but polite. Remember, the person who first reads the letter is most probably not the person who is to blame and is probably not the person who can actually resolve your problem.

Writing Resources
Unit 3

Photocopiable

Writing Resource 3A
Writing an article about a famous brand

Situation

You have been asked to write an article for a general interest magazine about a world famous brand, its image, and any relevant trademarks and logos.

Writing

A Choose a very well known brand and do some research into the origins, history, development, and current status of the brands and its associated trademarks and logos. Include information about how a particular brand came to exist. Also, if relevant, mention any problems or controversies that have arisen over the use of a certain logo, registered trademark, etc. Take notes and then start to arrange your notes under headings and in a logical sequence.

Brand: _____

Notes:

_____   _____
_____   _____
_____   _____
_____   _____
_____   _____

B Now start to compose sentences. Think about how to divide your writing into paragraphs and how to use connecting phrases to make your article easy for the general reader to understand.

C Write a first draft of your article. Check it and make corrections before writing out a final version.

Tips
■ Use a formal style. Do not use contractions or very colloquial expressions.
■ Use relatively simple language that can be understood by a layperson. Avoid using too much jargon and specialized technical terms.

Writing Resources
Unit 3

Photocopiable

Writing Resource 3B
Writing a marketing questionnaire

Situation

You work in the marketing department of a large company. You have been asked to prepare a series of questions for a questionnaire designed to elicit customers' reactions to one of the company's products or services.

Preparation

Choose ONE of the following products:
- cat food
- shampoo
- dry-cleaning services
- cable or satellite TV providers

Writing

A Decide which product or service to design your questionnaire about. Brainstorm initial ideas about the sort of information that would be useful for your company to know. Consider how often people buy your chosen product or service, what their expectations are, how they choose one product or service over another, etc. Take notes and then start to sort your ideas into groups.

Product / Service: _____

Find out:

_____   _____
_____   _____
_____   _____
_____   _____
_____   _____

B Now start to compose questions. Make sure that the questions are clear and unambiguous. Also, try to phrase the questions in such a way that the answers will not be vague and therefore of limited value.

Questions:

1. _____
2. _____
3. _____
4. _____
5. _____
6. _____
7. _____
8. _____

C Write a first draft of your questionnaire. Check it and make corrections before writing out a final version.

Tips
- Use clear, simple language that can be understood by a layperson.

Writing Resources
Unit 4
Photocopiable

Writing Resource 4A
Writing a letter of application for a study grant

Situation

Next year, you wish to study for a one-year MBA at an American university. Each year, the university offers a grant to a certain number of foreign students to cover the costs of their tuition and living expenses.

Preparation

Letters of application must be sent to Dean of the Business College, Mr. Paul Lindsay.

Writing

A Make notes of the content of your letter. Include the following points: Explain why you want to study for an MBA, outline the business area that interests you and why, and mention your long-term plans. Then start to arrange your notes into paragraphs in a logical sequence.

Notes:

_____   _____
_____   _____
_____   _____
_____   _____
_____   _____

B Arrange your letter according to standard conventions of format and layout.

> **Standard Conventions:**
> *At the start of your letter:* the relevant addresses, the date, and an appropriate salutation
> *At the end of your letter:* a suitable signing off phrase, your name, and your signature

C Write a first draft of your letter. Check it and make corrections before writing out a final version.

> **Tips**
> - Write in a formal register. Do not use contractions or colloquial expressions.
> - Adopt a tone that is positive and confident but that is not arrogant or "pushy".

Writing Resources

Unit 4

Photocopiable

Writing Resource 4B
Writing an article for the general reader

Situation

You have been asked to write an article for a general interest magazine describing and summarizing the key features of the economic system currently operating in your country.

Writing

A Look for information about the origins, history, and development of the economic system that predominates in your country. Include information about the balance between free-market activity and state-run businesses and deal with such matters as rates of inflation, imports and exports, interest rates, etc. Also, include information and your personal analysis and views on possible trends in the future. Take notes and then start to arrange your notes under headings and in a logical sequence.

Notes:

_____   _____
_____   _____
_____   _____
_____   _____
_____   _____

B Now start to compose sentences. Think about how to divide your writing into paragraphs and how to use connecting phrases to make your article easy for the general reader to understand.

C Write a first draft of your article. Check it and make corrections before writing out a final version.

Tips
■ Use a formal style. Do not use contractions or very colloquial expressions. ■ Use relatively simple language that can be understood by a layperson. Avoid using too much jargon and specialized technical terms.

Writing Resources
Unit 5

Photocopiable

Writing Resource 5A
Writing a personal letter to a friend or family member

Situation

A few months ago, you moved to another country for work. You are going to write a personal letter to a friend or family member in which you talk about how you are getting on and you relate your experiences adapting to life and work in your chosen country, which has a culture very different from that of your native country.

Writing

A Choose your foreign country and your field of work. Make notes about the sorts of contrasts that you have encountered on arriving in and adapting to a new country. These might include, the language, styles of greetings, the food, the weather, local customs, different work schedules, different attitudes towards punctuality, ways of doing business, etc. Also, include personal reflections on the things that have been the most interesting, the most surprising, the most difficult to get used to, etc.

B Make some rough notes and then start to organize your notes into categories and arrange them in a logical order.

Notes:

_____   _____
_____   _____
_____   _____
_____   _____
_____   _____

C Now start to compose sentences. Even though your letter is informal in style, think about how to divide it into paragraphs to make it easy for your reader to follow.

D Write a first draft of your letter. Check it and make corrections before writing out a final version.

Tips
■ In a personal letter, you can adopt a more relaxed style including contractions, abbreviations, and language of a less formal register.

Writing Resources
Unit 5

Photocopiable

Writing Resource 5B
Writing a report recommending a certain course of action

Situation

You are the general manager of an insurance company and you believe it is time that some of your company's tasks were outsourced to India. You are going to write a report to your CEO outlining why you believe this step is necessary.

Writing

A Brainstorm a list of reasons why you think some tasks should be outsourced to India. Make a list of advantages and benefits. Mention also any drawbacks that may have to be overcome in order for such an initiative to work.

Advantages:
_____
_____
_____
_____

Disadvantages:
_____
_____
_____
_____

B Make notes and then start to arrange these notes under headings and in a logical sequence. Bear in mind that the purpose of the report is to convince the reader of the validity of your arguments.

Use appropriate language to express necessity and obligation, that is, modal expressions such as *have to, need to, must, ought to, should,* etc.

C Arrange your report according to standard conventions of layout.

> **Writing a Report:**
> *Introduction:* The opening paragraph introduces the topic.
> *Body:* Each paragraph should contain and discuss an important point about your topic.
> *Conclusion:* The concluding paragraph should summarize important points in the report.

D Write a first draft of your report. Check it and make corrections before writing out a final version.

Tips
■ Write in a formal register. Do not use contractions or colloquial expressions.

Unit 1 Test

Test 1

Part 1 Complete the sentences with words from the box. There are two extra words. **(7 points)**

| experience | graduate | responsibilities | degree | candidates | position |
| references | | feature | commission | negotiation | |

Example: What qualifications are essential for the Accountant ____position____ ?

1. Does the Personnel Manager have to have a _____ ?
2. What _____ are listed for the Production Manager?
3. No previous _____ is necessary as on-the-job training is provided.
4. What _____ of the Financial Assistant job might motivate a candidate?
5. The company offers a basic salary and _____ on sales.
6. From the point of view of a new _____, what advantages does this job offer?
7. The _____ should have worked for at least three years for reputable companies.

Part 2 Match each verb with the correct noun or noun phrase. **(6 points)**

Example: follow ___e___   a. your abilities and skills

1. apply   _____   b. candidates
2. leave   _____   c. a decision
3. make   _____   d. an application form
4. short-list   _____   e. instructions
5. fill out   _____   f. a section blank
6. list   _____   g. for a job

Part 3 Complete each sentence with the correct form of *make* or *do*. **(6 points)**

Example: Try not to be nervous about the exams. Just ____do____ your best.

1. He _____ a very good impression when he went for the interview.
2. Later I realized that I _____ a big mistake in turning down their offer.
3. I'm _____ a course in time management. I'm finding it very useful.
4. Could you _____ me a favor? I need to print something and my printer isn't working.
5. After a difficult start, Julie is now _____ good progress in her job.
6. This company _____ a profit every year since 2001.

Part 4 Complete each sentence with the correct connector from the box. **(5 points)**

| however | but | since | also | so | though |

Example: ____Since____ he left college, he has been looking for work in real estate.

1. _____ she only graduated recently, she has already had some experience in sales.
2. I like solving problems. I _____ enjoy presenting new ideas to people.
3. I have never worked in insurance before and _____ this will be a new challenge for me.
4. Experience gives you an advantage _____ it is not a necessity.
5. Teamwork is important in this company. _____, you should also be able to work alone.

Part 5 In each sentence, underline the correct option. **(4 points)**

Example: Could you help me to (fill up / fill in for / <u>fill in</u>) this application form?

1. When Amy returned, we had to fill (her / her in / her up) on what had happened.
2. The conference room was empty when we arrived, but it soon filled (it up / in / up).
3. Alan is off sick today so I am filling (in for him / him in / up for him).
4. When there is not much to do, she fills (in / it in / up) her day with unnecessary phone calls.

Part 6 Listen to your teacher and complete the text. **(7 points)**

Good news! The selection ____committee____ has invited you for an interview. You don't have a lot of (1) _____ with interviews but you feel quite (2) _____. You're an extrovert and it should be easy to make a good (3) _____, right? But is it enough to wear your best clothes, smile pleasantly, and nod your head at the right times? Is it that easy? Well, not quite. (4) _____ has shown that job (5) _____ are often too complacent at interviews and that they come ill-prepared. Also, interviews can make even confident people feel (6) _____. You need to prepare yourself so that you can do your best. How can you prepare yourself? Ask yourself the following questions: Why do I want this job? What do I know about this company? Why do I want to work for this company? Why do I think I am the right person for this (7) _____?

108 Test

For Teacher's Use Only

Speaking

Photocopy these role cards and distribute both conversation 1 and 2 to the students. Allow a few minutes for them to prepare for their role plays. With a partner, have students role-play two telephone conversations based on the following information.

(15 points)

Conversation 1

Student A

You are a student counselor at a university. Call Student B (a student) to confirm the time of his/her appointment to talk about career choices.

Student B

You are a college student. Explain to the student counselor that you cannot go to your appointment because you are sick.

Conversation 2

Student A

You are a college student who cannot go to your appointment with the student counselor because you are sick. Call the university clinic and make an appointment to see the doctor.

Student B

You are a secretary at the university clinic. Take Student B's call and arrange a time for him/her to see the doctor.

Total points _____/50

Listening

Read the following passage aloud to the class.

Exercise 6
Good news! The selection committee has invited you for an interview. You don't have a lot of experience with interviews but you feel quite confident. You're an extrovert and it should be easy to make a good impression, right? But is it enough to wear your best clothes, smile pleasantly, and nod your head at the right times? Is it that easy? Well, not quite. Research has shown that job applicants are often too complacent at interviews and that they come ill-prepared. Also, interviews can make even confident people feel nervous. You need to prepare yourself so that you can do your best. How can you prepare yourself? Ask yourself the following questions: Why do I want this job? What do I know about this company? Why do I want to work for this company? Why do I think I am the right person for this position?

Unit 2

Part 1 Complete the present perfect sentences with the correct form of the given verb. **(7 points)**

Example: David _____has worked_____ (work) in London since 2002.

1. On-line travel booking _____ (change) the face of air travel.
2. Many companies _____ (benefit) enormously from the Internet.
3. Profits _____ (shoot) up in the last six months.
4. Independent travel _____ (grow) in recent years.
5. Sally _____ (be) Sales Director for two years.
6. I _____ (attend) six interviews in the past four days!
7. Competition _____ (increase) significantly since last year.

Part 2 Match the two halves of the conditional sentences. **(6 points)**

Example: If you want to take advantage of this offer,   __e__   a. then, yes, we're interested.

1. If you want people to remember your company, _____   b. they cost less.
2. If this plan can help to reduce our phone bills, _____   c. they come back again.
3. If you want to succeed in this career, _____   d. you don't run up a big debt.
4. If we make our calls at off-peak times, _____   e. call right away!
5. If you use your credit card responsibly, _____   f. give it a catchy name.
6. If you give people good service, _____   g. you have to work really hard.

Part 3 Complete each passive voice sentence with the correct form and tense of the given verb. **(7 points)**

Example: The order _____was placed_____ a month ago. (place / past)

1. A new sales record _____ last week. (break / past)
2. The shipment _____ to arrive on Thursday. (schedule / present)
3. The components _____ out last week. (send / past)
4. The appliances _____ in these special boxes. (pack / present)
5. Unfortunately, the parcel _____ somewhere in transit. (lose / past)
6. A special award _____ to the best employee. (give / present)
7. These products _____ all around the world. (sell / present)

Part 4 Complete each sentence with the correct form of a phrasal verb from the box. **(3 points)**

| turn out | pick up on | build on | tune into |

Example: A salesperson has to be able to ___tune into___ a customer's different needs and wants.

1. Are you good at _____ the subtle signals that people give?
2. We had some success last year. Now we need to _____ that this year.
3. Our marketing campaign is _____ to be a disaster!

Part 5 Complete the rewritten sentences using the given words. **(5 points)**

Example: Sales have increased dramatically. (dramatic)
There has been ___a dramatic increase in sales.___
1. There has been exponential growth in the number of franchises. (exponentially)
   The number of _____
2. Production fell catastrophically last year. (fall)
   There was _____
3. There was a steady increase in the number of complaints. (steadily)
   The number _____
4. The company's fortunes have declined rapidly in recent years. (rapid)
   There has _____
5. Profits dropped suddenly around March. (drop)
   There was _____

Part 6 Listen to your teacher and underline the correct options. **(7 points)**

   James Thompson grows organic vegetables. He used to sell (entirely / <u>exclusively</u>) to a large supermarket. One day, he had to request a (1) (delay / postponement) of a meeting with a buyer. The buyer arrogantly and rudely refused his (2) (request / demand). James felt angry at the supermarket and decided that he needed an (3) (unusual / alternative) sales outlet to make him more independent. He began to (4) (deliver / distribute) his vegetables door to door. That was 10 years ago and now the business has grown to 100 vans, 6 trucks, 35,000 boxes of vegetables a week, and 75,000 (5) (consumers / customers). Guy believes his business gives people what they really want—(6) (nourishing / healthy), homegrown, tasty organic vegetables. His selling (7) (advantage / benefit) over supermarkets is speed and freshness. His vegetables are on the customer's doorstep 24 to 48 hours after being harvested.

For Teacher's Use Only

Speaking

Photocopy these role cards and distribute to the students. Allow a few minutes for them to prepare for their role plays. With a partner, have students role-play a conversation based on the following information.

(15 points)

Student A

You are a salesperson with a lot of experience, especially in two specific types of sales. At various times, you have sold things door to door and you have sold things over the phone. With Student B, another experienced salesperson, discuss the advantages and disadvantages of different types of sales jobs.

Student B

You are a salesperson with a lot of experience, especially in two specific types of sales. At various times, you have sold things in the street and you have worked as a salesperson in a department store. With Student A, another experienced salesperson, discuss the advantages and disadvantages of different types of sales jobs.

Total points _____ /50

Listening

Read the following passage aloud to the class.

Exercise 6

James Thompson grows organic vegetables. He used to sell exclusively to a large supermarket. One day, he had to request a postponement of a meeting with a buyer. The buyer arrogantly and rudely refused his request. James felt angry at the supermarket and decided that he needed an alternative sales outlet to make him more independent. He began to deliver his vegetables door to door. That was 10 years ago and now the business has grown to 100 vans, 6 trucks, 35,000 boxes of vegetables a week, and 75,000 customers. Guy believes his business gives people what they really want—healthy, homegrown, tasty organic vegetables. His selling advantage over supermarkets is speed and freshness. His vegetables are on the customer's doorstep 24 to 48 hours after being harvested.

Unit 3

Part 1 Complete each space in the text with the passive voice (present) form of one of the verbs in the box.
(6 points)

| take | keep | pass | pay | use | recommend | sell |

Advertising ____is used____ by almost every company that produces goods or provides a service. The object of an ad is to convince people to take some action that (1) _____ by the advertiser. Just like salespeople, ads try to persuade, but final decisions (2) _____ by the customer. With advertising, companies enjoy the economies of mass selling and some of these economies (3) _____ on to consumers. Thus, products that (4) _____ mainly through advertising are usually cheaper. Through advertising, the public (5) _____ informed about new products. Also, many TV and radio shows (6) _____ for by advertising.

Part 2 In each sentence, underline the correct word to complete the compound adjective. . **(5 points)**

Example: Years of trouble (-lasting / -*free* / -purpose) cleaning-guaranteed!

1. The book contains recipes for hundreds of mouth (-lasting / -saving / -watering) dishes.
2. This is one of the most well (-friendly / -saving / -known) products on the market.
3. One thing I like about this product is that it is very user (-known / -friendly / -purpose).
4. The family (-purpose / -size / -cutting) package offers exceptional value!
5. Look at these fantastic space (-saving / -lasting / -watering) features!

Part 3 Complete each space in the comparative sentences with just one word. **(5 points)**

Example: Organic food is healthier ____*than*____ non-organic food.

1. In my opinion, Italian cooking is _____ good _____ French cooking.
2. In gas consumption, hybrid cars are _____ economical _____ conventional cars.
3. These imported laptops are _____ cheap _____ the ones made in this country.
4. For me, this cheese is better _____ that one because it is fat-free.
5. These new shoes are _____ comfortable _____ my old ones.

Part 4 Complete each sentence with the correct tense (*present perfect* or *past simple*) of the verb. **(5 points)**

Example: Keith ____*completed*____ (complete) his MBA in 2003.

1. Sales _____ (be) very good since we changed our advertising strategy.
2. Last week, they _____ (have) a meeting and came up with a new plan.
3. Samantha _____ (start) her own company three years ago.
4. Since we launched our web site, we _____ (see) a big increase in demand.
5. I _____ (work) on three advertising campaigns so far.

Part 5 Complete each sentence with the correct connecting word or phrase from the box. **(4 points)**

consequently	since	because	due to	and so

Example: Pirated goods often look exactly like the originals ____*and so*____ it is hard to spot the fakes.

1. _____ pirated goods are cheaper than originals, consumers can save a lot of money.
2. Famous brands are very fashionable and, _____, these are the ones that are copied.
3. _____ the fact that handbags are important accessories, there is a big demand for fakes.
4. Famous brands are copied the most _____ they are symbols of luxury and status.

Part 6 Write the correct noun or adjective. **(5 points)**

	Noun	**Adjective**
Example:	revolution	*revolutionary*
1.	_____	special
2.	innovation	_____
3.	_____	strategic
4.	durability	_____
5.	_____	persuasive

Part 7 Listen to your teacher. Read the sentences. Circle True or False. **(5 points)**

1. Mr. Steiner works for a company called Insight.   True   False
2. Mr. Steiner was in a meeting when Mr. Schroeder called.   True   False
3. Mr. Schroeder wants to talk about some changes to some designs.   True   False
4. Mr. Schroeder wants to have a meeting on Wednesday morning.   True   False
5. Mr. Steiner suggested a lunchtime meeting.   True   False

For Teacher's Use Only

Speaking

Photocopy these role cards and distribute to the students. Allow a few minutes for them to prepare for their role plays. With a partner, have students role-play a conversation based on one of the following situations.

(15 points)

Conversation 1

Student A

You are an employee at a large company. You have been asked to attend a meeting of the marketing department but you cannot go. Call the Marketing Manager's personal assistant (Student B) and explain and offer your apologies for missing the meeting.

Student B

You are the personal assistant to the Marketing Manager. Take a telephone call from Student A and explain to him/her that the Marketing Manager is very busy and will not be able to meet until at least two weeks from now.

Conversation 2

Student A

You are an employee at a large company. You need to have a meeting in the next week with the Marketing Manager about a product that is about to be launched. Call the Marketing Manager's personal assistant (Student B) and request a meeting.

Student B

You are the personal assistant to the Marketing Manager. Take a telephone call from Student A and explain to him/her that the Marketing Manager thinks that it is very important that he/she attends next week's marketing meeting.

Total points _____/50

Listening

Read the following passages aloud to the class.

Exercise 7
Mr. Steiner, while you were in the meeting, a Mr. Schroeder called – Jeff Schroeder. He's from that design company called Insight. He said that he would like to meet with you on Wednesday afternoon to talk about some changes to some designs. I told him you were busy on Wednesday afternoon. I suggested Wednesday morning but he can't make it then. He suggested a lunchtime meeting on Wednesday before your meeting. He says he needs you to get back to him today. What should I tell him?

Test 115

Unit 4

Part 1 Complete each sentence with a word from the box. There is one extra word. **(6 points)**

| balance sheet | debtor | fixed assets | inflation |
| liabilities | capital | creditor | current assets |

Example: Current and fixed debts and expenses that must be paid are called ___liabilities___.

1. A _____ is a statement showing the financial position of a business.
2. The assets that a business has and uses over a long period of time are called _____.
3. A _____ is a person, group, or organization to whom money is owed.
4. The rate of _____ shows how the prices of goods increase over time.
5. Assets that can change from day to day are called _____.
6. Accumulated wealth especially money used to produce more wealth is called _____.

Part 2 Read the text and number the lines in the correct order. **(6 points)**

_____ of prices causing or caused by an increase in the supply of money or by
_____ with this steady rate of inflation since they receive an annual pay rise.
_____ an expansion in the economy. When interest rates go up and the cost of
_____ can result. For the last thirty years or so, the average rate of inflation
__1__ Inflation is a substantial and continuing overall rise in the general level
_____ in the US has been steady at about 3% a year. Most people can cope
_____ borrowing increases, the cost of running a business increases and inflation

Part 3 Match the two halves of the sentences. **(5 points)**

Example: Competition hit commissions and this ___b___   a. boosted gas production.
1. P&H recovered slightly last year but then _____   b. caused futures trading profits to fall.
2. Omega's acquisition of Eastern Energy _____   c. put shareholders through the wringer.
3. The market's volatile behavior recently _____   d. suffered a loss of $6 million.
4. Frood's strong sales in all areas _____   e. created very high postal costs.
5. The company offered free delivery and this _____   f. helped them turn in solid Q1 figures.

Part 4 Complete each question with the correct word. **(6 points)**

Example: ____What____ is the current level of inflation in your country?

1. _____ often can I view my account online?
2. _____ there 24-hour customer service available?
3. _____ won't Steve rent a place of his own this year?
4. Is _____ possible to transfer funds electronically?
5. _____ of his expenses does Andy intend to eliminate completely?
6. _____ can I talk to about my financial problems?

Part 5 In each sentence, underline the correct option. **(6 points)**

Example: Are these fixed expenses or (varied / <u>variable</u>) expenses?

1. Yes, we are facing some (liquid / liquidity) problems but this is just temporary – we hope.
2. The (volatility / volatile) of some exchange rates makes it hard to say how things will develop.
3. You want my advice? Buy some (stock / stock market) in a successful software company.
4. You should keep some low-risk savings income as a (hedging / hedge) against market changes.
5. I try to maintain a (diversify / diversified) portfolio in case the market changes suddenly.
6. The investigation for alleged (fraud / fraudulent) has caused a scandal in the industry.

Part 6 Listen to your teacher. Read the sentences. Circle True or False. **(6 points)**

Example: Bartering is a new concept.   True   <u>False</u>

1. In 1935, Monsanto bought saccharin from a Chinese company.   True   False
2. Monsanto accepted the mackerel because the company could not pay cash.   True   False
3. PepsiCo did a deal with the Russian government in 1962.   True   False
4. Pepsi received vodka instead of Russian rubles.   True   False
5. The Thai government swapped 300,000 tons of rice for 60,000 cattle.   True   False
6. By bartering, the Thai government avoided a big drop in the price of rice.   True   False

For Teacher's Use Only

Speaking

Photocopy these role cards and distribute to the students. Allow a few minutes for them to prepare for their role plays. With a partner, have students role-play a conversation based on the following information.

(15 points)

Student A

You are a student interested in having a credit card. Ask Student B, a bank employee, about how to obtain a credit card. Ask for information about different types of accounts and about interest rates and charges.

Student B

You are a bank employee. Give information to Student A about the different types of credit cards and different types of interest. Explain about charges and benefits. Give advice on sensible credit card use.

Total points _____ /50

Listening

Read the following passage aloud to the class.

Exercise 6

Whether it is a large company with excess stock or a small business that needs to grow but does not have the cash, barter offers a way out of a fix. Bartering is as old as trading and corporate barter is not a new idea either.

In 1935, US pharmaceutical giant Monsanto sold saccharin to a company in China. When the company was unable to pay in cash, Monsanto took frozen mackerel in exchange and acquired an export market in the most populous country in the world.

In 1972, PepsiCo did a deal with the government of the USSR to supply the first western consumer product on sale in the Soviet Union. Instead of roubles, Pepsi was traded for vodka and PepsiCo acquired distribution rights to Stolichnaya in the US.

And massive swap deals still happen today. Recently, the Thai government agreed to arrange a swap of 60,000 tons of excess rice for 300,000 South African cattle, thus avoiding a drop in rice prices and solving its beef shortage in one single trade. And thousands of small firms are also finding barter an indispensable part of their business.

Unit 5

Part 1 Complete each sentence with the correct phrasal verb from the box. **(5 points)**

| catch on | get in on | turn out | tune in | work out | get on |

Example: It takes a while before you start to really _____tune in_____ to how other people think.

1. Sure, we get discouraged sometimes, but we just have to _____ with the job.
2. I didn't _____ at first. I didn't realize that they were only joking.
3. We're disappointed because the project didn't _____ as well as we had hoped.
4. He's impatient to start and _____ all the action.
5. When I first arrived, it took me a while to _____ how everything was organized.

Part 2 Underline the correct opposite of each adjective. **(7 points)**

Example: proper   a. non-proper   b. unproper   c. improper

1. existent   a. unexistent   b. non-existent   c. inexistent
2. lawful   a. non-lawful   b. unlawful   c. illawful
3. logical   a. non-logical   b. unlogical   c. illogical
4. rational   a. irrational   b. non-rational   c. unrational
5. profitable   a. improfitable   b. unprofitable   c. non-profitable
6. prudent   a. unprudent   b. non-prudent   c. imprudent
7. discriminatory   a. non-discriminatory b. undiscriminatory   c. indiscriminatory

Part 3 Complete each sentence with a connecting word or phrase from the box. **(5 points)**

| however | as a result | consequently | apart from | not only | instead |

Example: Graduates want to be part of the global economy. _____Consequently_____, they must know English.

1. _____ of working here before I start college, I want to get a job in Australia.
2. I found a great website. _____ does it explain grammar, but also English idioms.
3. Nobody here speaks her language. _____, she's finding it hard to cope with it all.
4. There are many language schools. _____, not all of them have official recognition.
5. _____ improving his global knowledge, learning English will improve his chances of getting a place at university.

Test 119

Part 4 Read the text. Rewrite the reported speech sentences in direct speech. **(5 points)**

Dave told me about alternative energy sources. He said that once a nuclear power plant was set up, energy was constant and cheap. He said that solar panel installation was expensive but the cost would drop as demand increased. He told me that biomass was an efficient way of using waste and it could reduce pollution. He explained that the problem with hydrogen was that it had to be made. He said that wind power had limitations because it required a certain volume and velocity. He told me that, economically, biomass was not cost effective as it contained less energy per kilo than fossil fuels.

Example: "Once a nuclear power *plant is set up, energy is constant and cheap.*"

1. "Solar panel installation _____
2. "Biomass _____
3. "The problem with hydrogen _____
4. "Wind power _____
5. "Economically, biomass _____

Part 5 Complete the sentences with the correct present passive voice forms. **(7 points)**

Example: If commodity prices drop, farmers' income ____*is affected*____ (affect) seriously.

1. Often, workers in developing countries _____ (pay) very low wages.
2. Poorer countries suffer when profits _____ (take) out of the country.
3. Ethical trade is about how goods are produced and how they _____ (sell).
4. Fairtrade labeled products _____ (find) in many large supermarkets.
5. The benefits of free trade _____ (bring) to the people who need it most.
6. Fairtrade guarantees that a farmer _____ (give) a fair deal.
7. However world prices are at the time, production costs _____ (cover).

Part 6 Listen to your teacher and complete the text. **(6 points)**

In today's global economy, ____*diversity*____ has become the norm. In some workplaces, there can be employees of over twenty-five different (1) _____. The issue is how to accommodate the (2) _____ views about life and the world that such a multi-ethnic (3) _____ creates. A harmonious (4) _____ is vital to the maintenance of a healthy workplace. If this is not the case, productivity can suffer and a high staff (5) _____ rate may affect profits and morale. Diversity training began in the USA in the early 1990's and since that time, there has been a huge increase in the number of (6) _____, courses, videos and books about how to deal with diversity in the workplace.

Test

For Teacher's Use Only

Speaking

Photocopy these role cards and distribute to the students. Allow a few minutes for them to prepare for their role plays. With a partner, have students role-play a conversation based on the following information.

(15 points)

Student A

You are a foreigner who has just moved to this country. You have never been here before and you need some advice about cultural matters. Ask Student B for advice about how to behave. Ask about time-keeping, dress codes, food habits, greetings, tipping in restaurants, etc.

Student B

Answer Student A's questions about your country. Add further advice of your own.

Total points ____/50

Listening

Read the following passages aloud to the class.

Exercise 6

In today's global economy, diversity has become the norm. In some workplaces, there can be employees of over twenty-five different nationalities. The issue is how to accommodate the diverse views about life and the world that such a multi-ethnic environment creates. A harmonious atmosphere is vital to the maintenance of a healthy workplace. If this is not the case, productivity can suffer and a high staff turnover rate may affect profits and morale. Diversity training began in the USA in the early 1990's and since that time, there has been a huge increase in the number of consultants, courses, videos and books about how to deal with diversity in the workplace.

Tests 1-5 — Answer Key

Test 1

1 1. degree 2. responsibilities 3. experience 4. feature 5. commission 6. graduate 7. candidates

2 1. g 2. f 3. c 4. b 5. d, 6. a

3 1. made 2. had made 3. doing 4. do 5. making 6. has made

4 1. though 2. also 3. so 4. but 5. however

5 1. her in 2. up 3. in for him 4. up

6 1. experience 2. confident 3. impression 4. Research 5. applicants 6. nervous 7. position

Test 2

1 1. has changed 2. have benefited 3. have shot 4. has grown 5. has been 6. have attended 7. has increased

2 1. f 2. a 3. g 4. b 5. d 6. c

3 1. was broken 2. is scheduled 3. were sent 4. are packed 5. was lost 6. is given 7. are sold

4 1. picking up on 2. build on 3. turning out

5 1. The number of franchises has grown exponentially. 2. There was a catastrophic fall in production last year. 3. The number of complaints increased steadily. 4. There has been a rapid decline in the company's fortunes in recent years. 5. There was a sudden drop in profits around March.

6 1. postponement 2. request 3. alternative 4. deliver 5. customers 6. healthy 7. advantage

Test 3

1 1. is recommended 2. are taken 3. are passed 4. are sold 5. is informed 6. are paid

2 1. mouth-watering 2. well-known 3. user-friendly 4. family-size 5. space-saving

3 1. not / as 2. more / than 3. as / as 4. than 5. not / as

4 1. have been 2. had 3. started 4. have seen 5. have worked

5 1. since 2. consequently 3. due to 4. because

6 1. specialty 2. innovative 3. strategy 4. durable 5. persuasion

7 1. False 2. True 3. True 4. False 5. False

Tests 1-5 — Answer Key

Test 4

1 1. balance sheet 2. fixed assets 3. creditor 4. inflation 5. current assets 6. capital

2 Inflation is a substantial and continuing overall rise in the general level of prices causing or caused by an increase in the supply of money or by an expansion in the economy. When interest rates go up and the cost of borrowing increases, the cost of running a business increases and inflation can result. For the last thirty years or so, the average rate of inflation in the US has been steady at about 3% a year. Most people can cope with this steady rate of inflation since they receive an annual pay rise.

3 1. d 2. a 3. c 4. f 5. e

4 1. How 2. Is 3. Why 4. it 5. Which 6. Who

5 1. liquidity 2. volatility 3. stock 4. hedge 5. diversified 6. fraud

6 1. False 2. True 3. False 4. True 5. False 6. True

Test 5

1 1. get on 2. catch on 3. turn out 4. get in on 5. work out

2 1. b 2. b 3. c 4. a 5. b 6. c 7. a

3 1. instead 2. not only 3. as a result 4. however 5. apart from

4 1. "Solar panel installation is expensive but the cost will drop as demand increases." 2. "Biomass is an efficient way of using waste and it can reduce pollution." 3. "The problem with hydrogen is that it has to be made." 4. "Wind power has limitations because it requires a certain volume and velocity." 5. "Economically, biomass is not cost effective as it contains less energy per kilo than fossil fuels."

5 1. are paid 2. are taken 3. are sold 4. are found 5. are brought 6. is given 7. are covered

6 1. nationalities 2. diverse 3. environment 4. atmosphere 5. turnover 6. consultants